Crossword Puzzles for Kids Ages 8 to 12

90 Crossword Easy Puzzles

This book includes free bonus that are available here:
www.funspace.club
Follow us: facebook.com/funspaceclub

Introduction

This crosswords puzzle book contain English words for kids 8-12 years olds. Crosswords is a very easy and simple game. It's fun & educate kids. You just have to have a good stock of words. Look at empty boxes. By default, the game takes you through the clues in order starting with clue 1. After you fill in a clue you are taken to the next one. You have to fill up those across (horizontal) empty boxes and down (vertical) empty boxes with the right words and phrases by using clue to get idea.

See more great books for kids at

www.funspace.club
Follow us : facebook.com/funspaceclub

Send email to get answer & solution here : funspaceclub18@gmail.com

ADJECTIVES

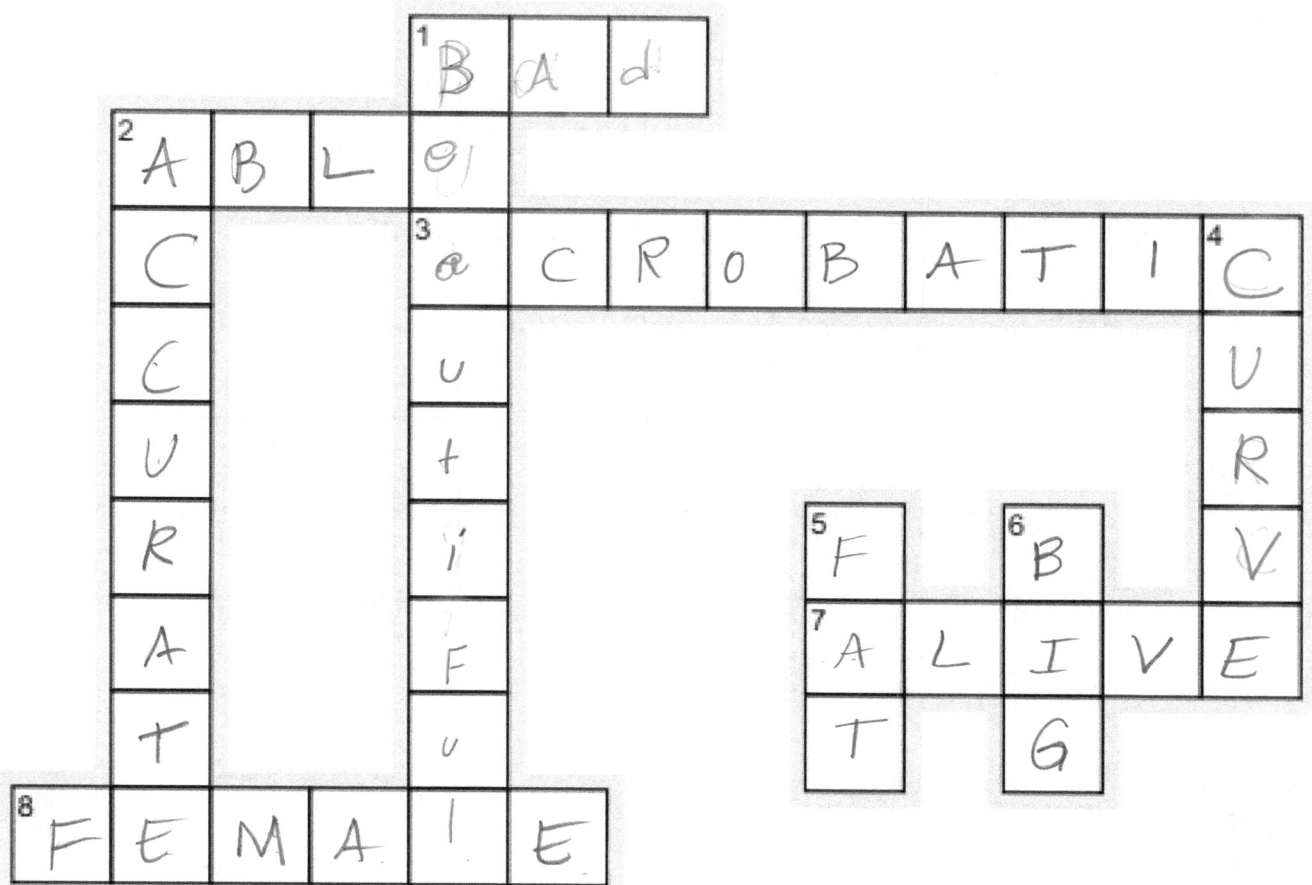

Across

1. Having undesirable or negative qualities
2. Having the skill or power needed to do a thing.
3. Having to do with acrobats or feats of balance and skill.
7. Having life; living.
8. Characteristic of or peculiar to a woman

Down

1. Delightful to see, hear, or experience; lovely to the senses; having beauty.
2. Free of mistakes or error; conforming exactly or almost exactly to fact or to a standard or performing with total accuracy.
4. A line that bends smoothly in one direction without any straight parts or angles.
5. Having an (over)abundance of flesh
6. Large in size, number, or weight.

AIR TRAVEL

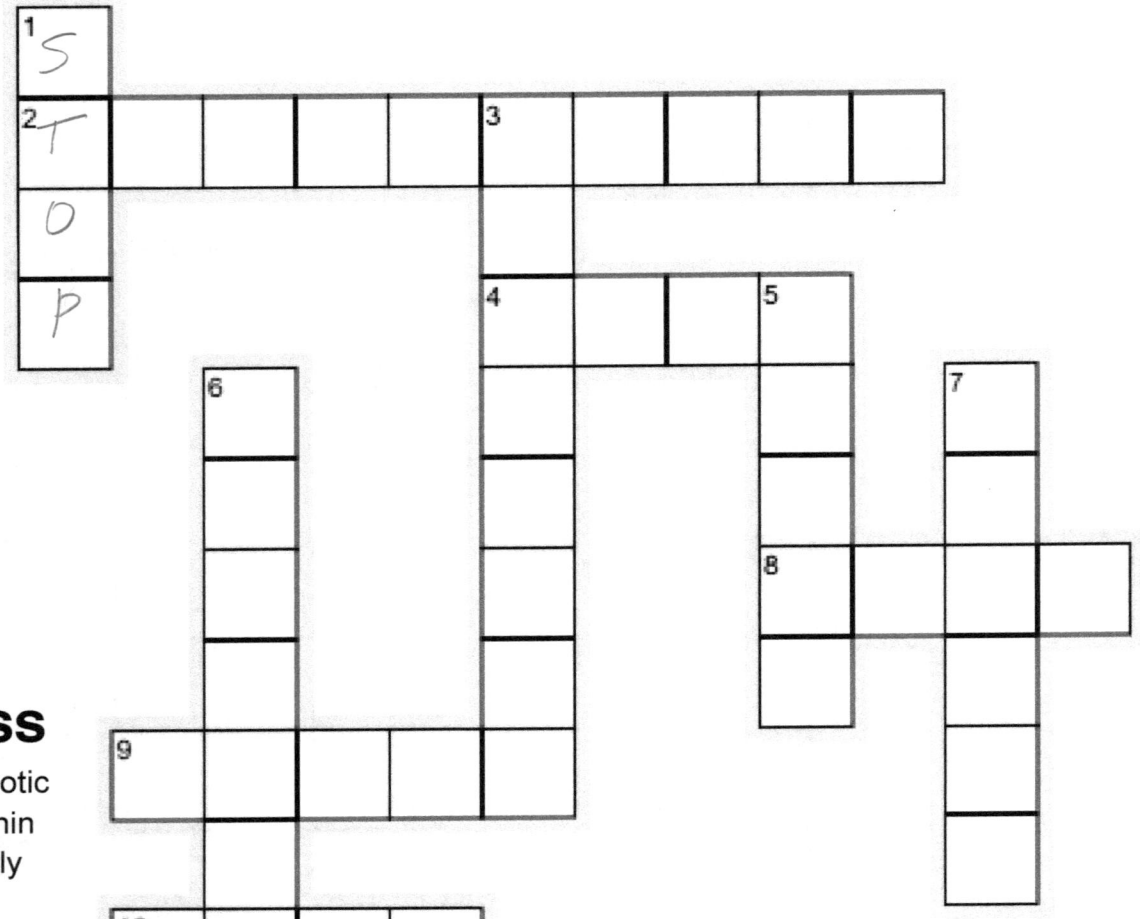

1 S
2 T
3
O
P
4 **5**
6 **7**
8
9
10 S E A T

Across

2. The chaotic motion within some swiftly moving or changing air or water currents.
4. Permission granted by an appropriate national official, and so indicated on a passport, that its bearer may travel within that nation.
8. (Air travel) cause to come to the ground
9. _____-on - of luggage, small enough to be stored in the passenger cabin of an airplane.
10. _____ belt - a strap or belt that holds a person in the seat of a car, airplane, or other vehicle. They protect people against a sudden stop or crash.

Down

1. _____ over - to make a brief stop before traveling further.
3. A room with sinks and toilets.
5. An open space for passing between rows or sections of seats or shelves.
6. Suitcases, boxes, and bags for carrying one's things on trips; baggage.
7. A smooth, level strip on which airplanes take off and land.

ANIMALS

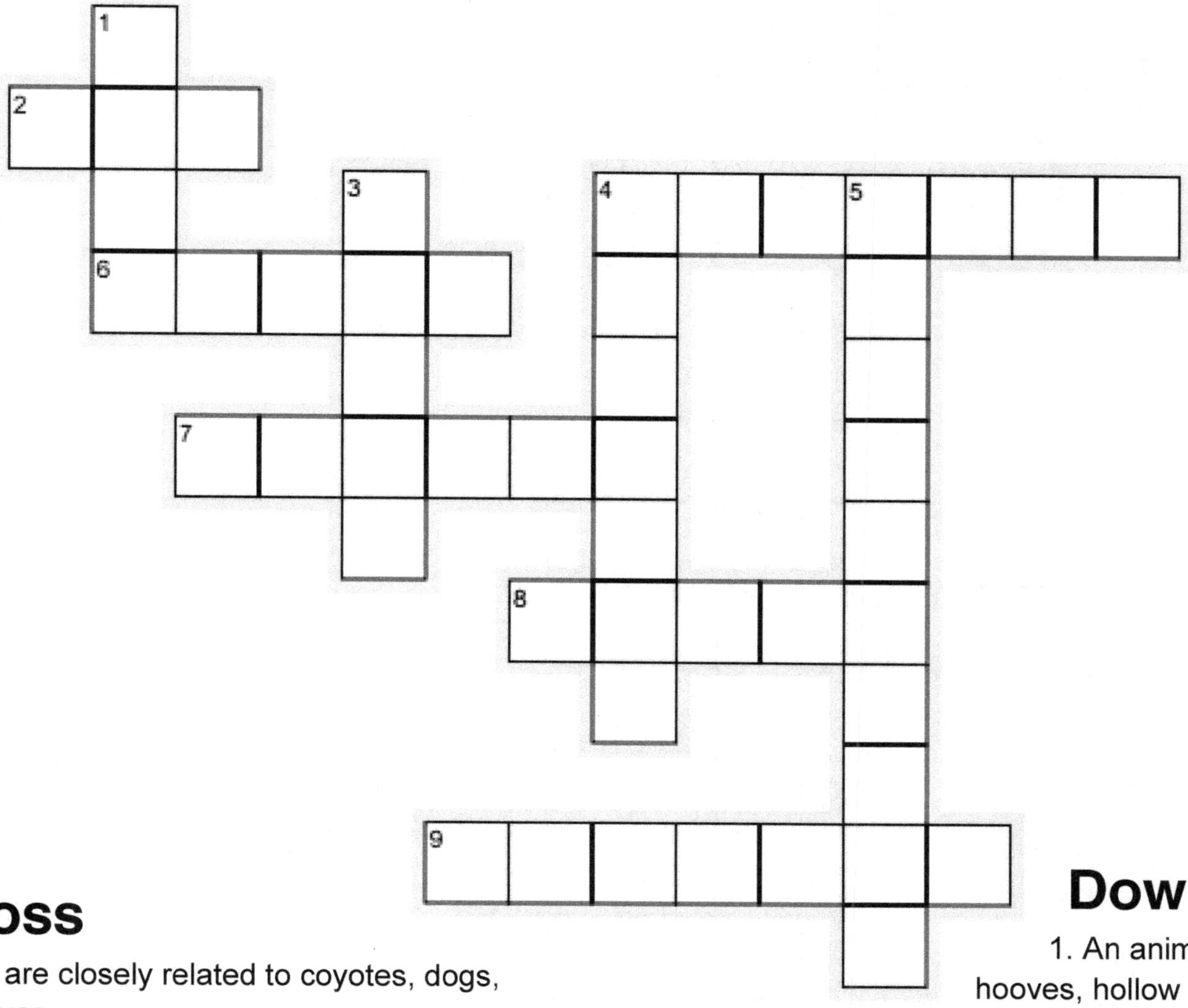

Across

2. They are closely related to coyotes, dogs, and wolves.
4. A common farm bird that is raised for its meat and eggs.
6. They are the largest of the big cats and are closely related to lions, leopards, and other cats that roar.
7. A reptile with a soft body covered by a hard shell that lives in water or on land. It pulls its head, legs, and tail into its shell for protection.
8. A large black-and-white mammal that is related to bears.
9. An animal with a hard, jointed shell that lives in the ocean. They have four pairs of legs and a pair of large claws.

Down

1. An animal with hooves, hollow horns, and rough hair. They are mammals that are raised for their milk, wool, and meat. They are closely related to sheep.
3. A large mammal with a striped coat, long legs, and hooves. They are closely related to horses but have shorter manes.
4. A large, wild cat of Africa and southern Asia that has solid black spots on its fur. They have long legs and are the fastest animal on land. Sometimes they are trained for hunting game.
5. A mammal that lives in African rain forests. They are in the group of primate mammals called apes.

ANTONYMS

Across

1. Opposite of the word "disadvantage".
3. Opposite of the word "defeat".
5. Opposite of the word "outside".
6. Opposite of the word "peace".
7. Opposite of the word "scarce".
8. Opposite of the word "strong".

Down

2. Opposite of the word "inaccurate".
4. Opposite of the word "invisible".
5. Opposite of the word "narrow".
6. Opposite of the word "right".

APRIL FOOL'S DAY

Across

2. A plan or plot.
3. A gullible person; one who can be readily misled or fooled.
5. The fourth month of the year. It has thirty days.
6. Extremely wrong or harmful.

Down

1. Living in a natural state; not tamed.
2. To catch (someone or something) off guard; act upon without giving any warning.
4. Not having good sense; silly.
7. Something done to fool or cheat someone.
8. To bother or disturb with irritating behavior.
9. A dishonest, often elaborate, business scheme that uses deception to obtain money, often employing the telephone or Internet to reach a large number of people.

ASTRONOMY

Across

1. The curved path in space that is followed by an object going round and round a planet, moon, or star.

3. A dwarf planet that is usually farther from the Sun than any of the planets (It was considered to be a planet until 2006).

6. _____ Tiny planet that mostly orbit between Mars and Jupiter.

7. Is a reddish planet and the fourth planet from the sun. It is the planet that comes closest to the Earth.

9. A meteor that has fallen to Earth. They are made of stone, iron, or stony-iron.

Down

2. The Earth is _____s of years old; A thousand million.

4. It is an enormous group of stars.

5. A cloud of gas and dust in space.

7. The object that you can often see in the sky at night.

8. Asteroid _____ - is a doughnut-shaped concentration of asteroids that orbit the Sun between the orbits of Mars and Jupiter.

BEACH

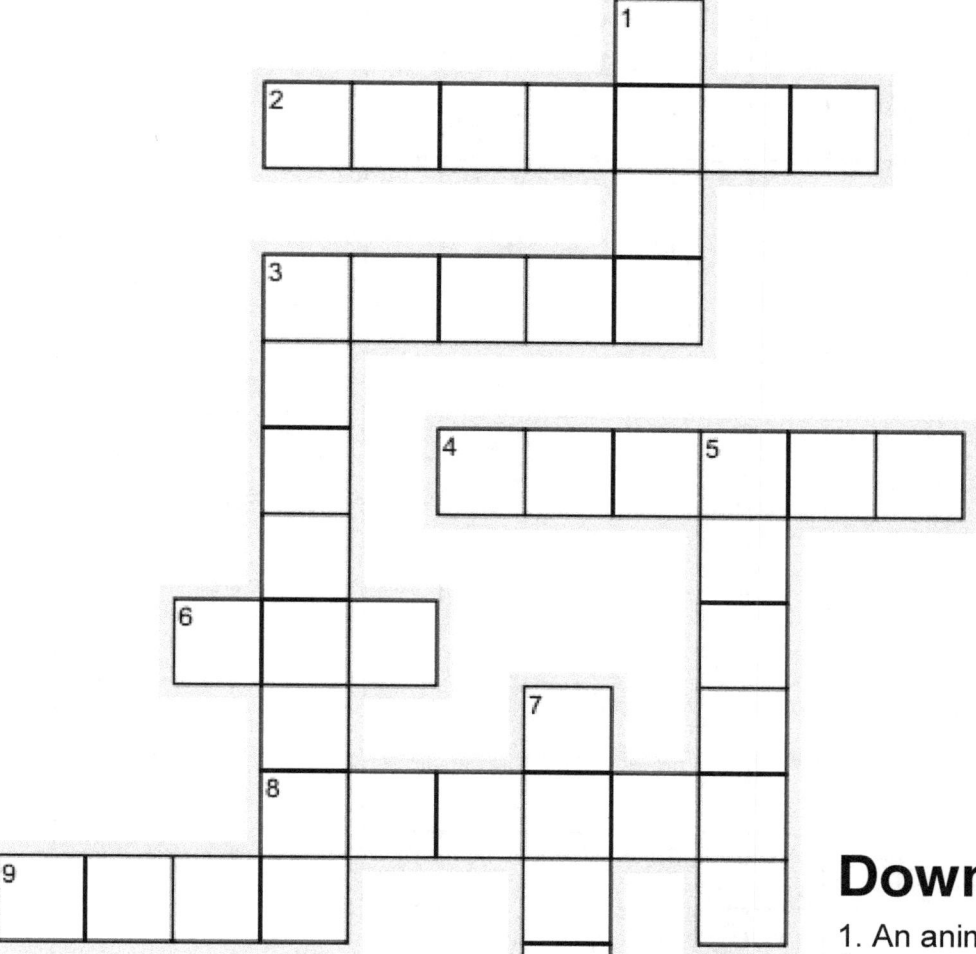

Across

2. _____ suit - A garment worn for swimming.
3. _____ ball - A large inflatable ball of brightly colored plastic, usu. used for games played in or near the water.
4. A very brief, two-piece bathing suit for women, or underpants cut like the bottom half of this bathing suit.
6. A part of a sea or lake that cuts into a coastline and is partly surrounded by land.
8. A shallow body of salt water by the sea. It is separated from the sea by sandbars, coral reefs, or islands.
9. A small bay.

Down

1. An animal that lives in water and has fins for swimming and gills for breathing.
3. A small sea animal that attaches its shell to rocks, the bottom of ships, docks, and other objects in shallow parts of the ocean. They float freely in the ocean when they are young. They develop shells with sharp edges as adults. They are kinds of crustaceans.
5. An area of land smaller than a continent and surrounded by water on all sides.
7. The hard skeleton of tiny sea animals. Most of them live in warm tropical oceans, and their thousands of skeletons form reefs and atolls.

BIRTHDAY

Across

3. A small, thin, rubber bag that you blow air into so that it becomes larger and rounder or longer.
4. A two wheeled vehicle to move around on that uses the feet to make it move.
7. Something that you give someone as a present.
9. A pretty loop of ribbon to decorate a present.
10. Young people.

Down

1. The action of expelling air from the mouth.
2. The act of looking forward and being excited about an event.
5. Candy on a stick.
6. Something that is suitable and correct for the occasion.
8. A small, hand-held firework that throws off sparks when lit.

BODY

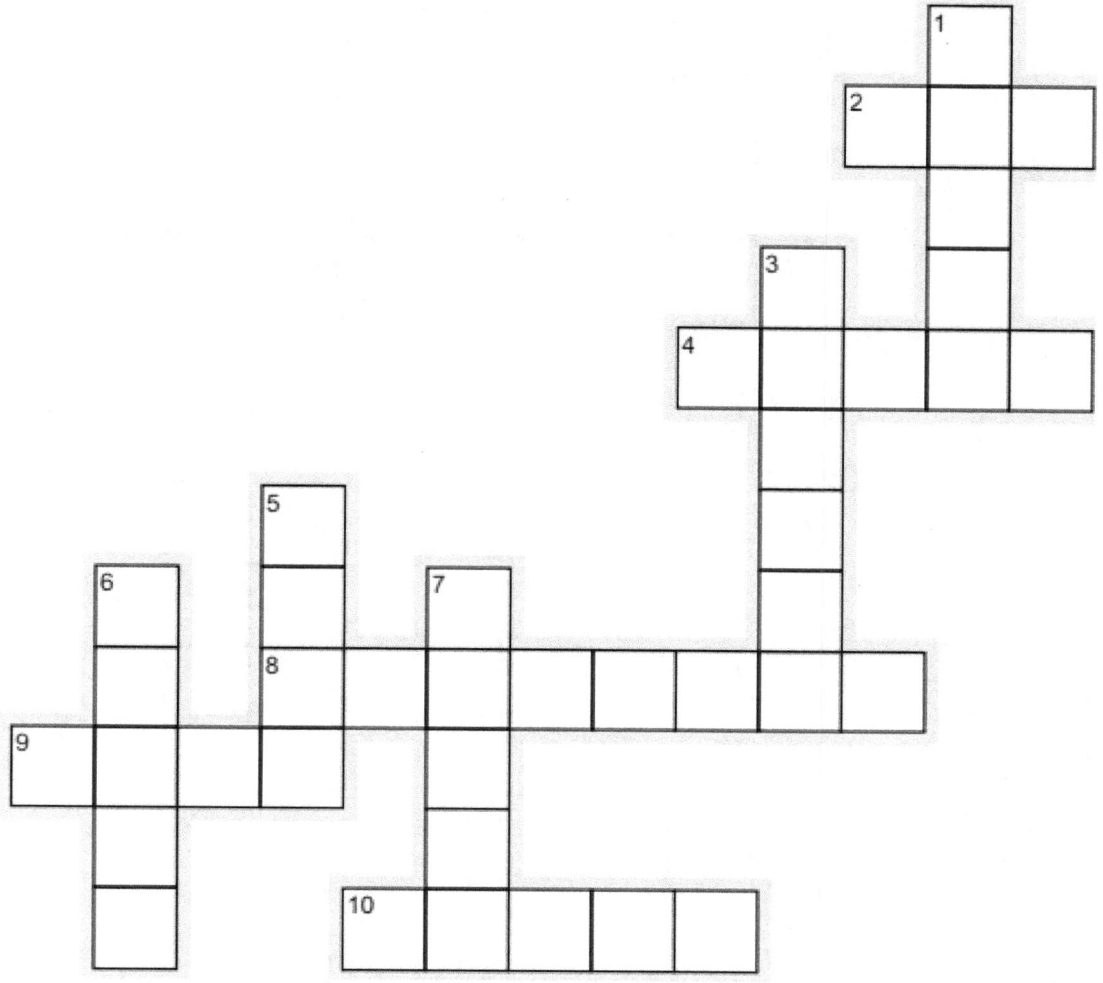

Across

2. The part of the human body between the shoulder and the wrist.
4. Hard, white, bony objects that grow in rows in the jaws of people and animals. They are used for biting and chewing.
8. The part of the human body between the neck and the upper arm.
9. The hard tissue that forms the skeleton of a person or animal.
10. The hair growing on a man's face.

Down

1. The joint between the arm and hand, or the bones that make up this joint.
3. The movable organ in the bottom of the mouth, used for licking, tasting, swallowing, and human speech.
5. The part of the face on people and certain animals through which they breathe and smell.
6. The red liquid containing oxygen and nutrients that pumps through the veins and arteries of humans and many other animals.
7. The sounds produced through the mouth by a human being.

ADJECTIVES

Across

2. To surprise greatly or fill with wonder; astonish.
4. Pleasant, nice, or likable; Conforming to your own liking, feelings or nature
5. Easy to bend or to shape; not firm or hard.
7. Close to the ground or bottom; not high.
9. Costing a lot of money; having a high price.
10. Being free from sickness; well; fit.

Down

1. Fastened or shut in a secure way; fixed in place.
3. Having or showing a strong desire to succeed; having ambition.
6. Feeling joy or pleasure; being glad or content.
8. Having a great amount of money or valuable property

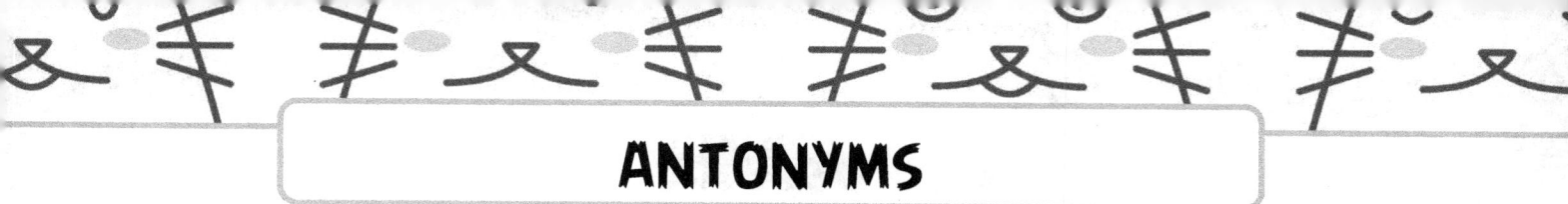

ANTONYMS

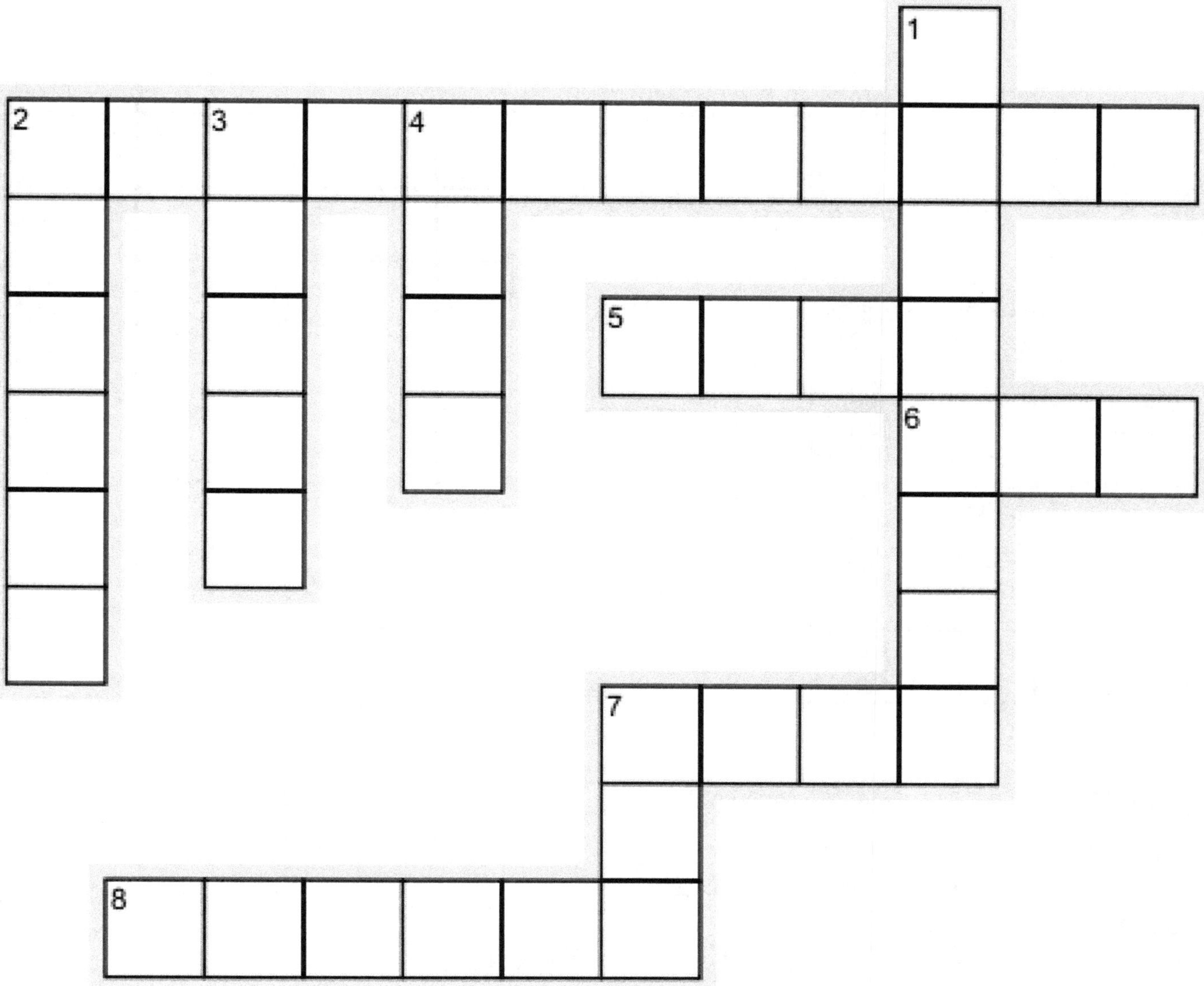

Across

2. Opposite of the word "unsatisfactory".
5. Opposite of the word "opposite".
6. Opposite of the word "bottom".
7. Opposite of the word "sweet".
8. Opposite of the word "joy".

Down

1. Opposite of the word "apart".
2. _____ - hand - Opposite of the word "brand new".
3. Opposite of the word "easy".
4. Opposite of the word "none".
7. Opposite of the word "reap".

BEACH

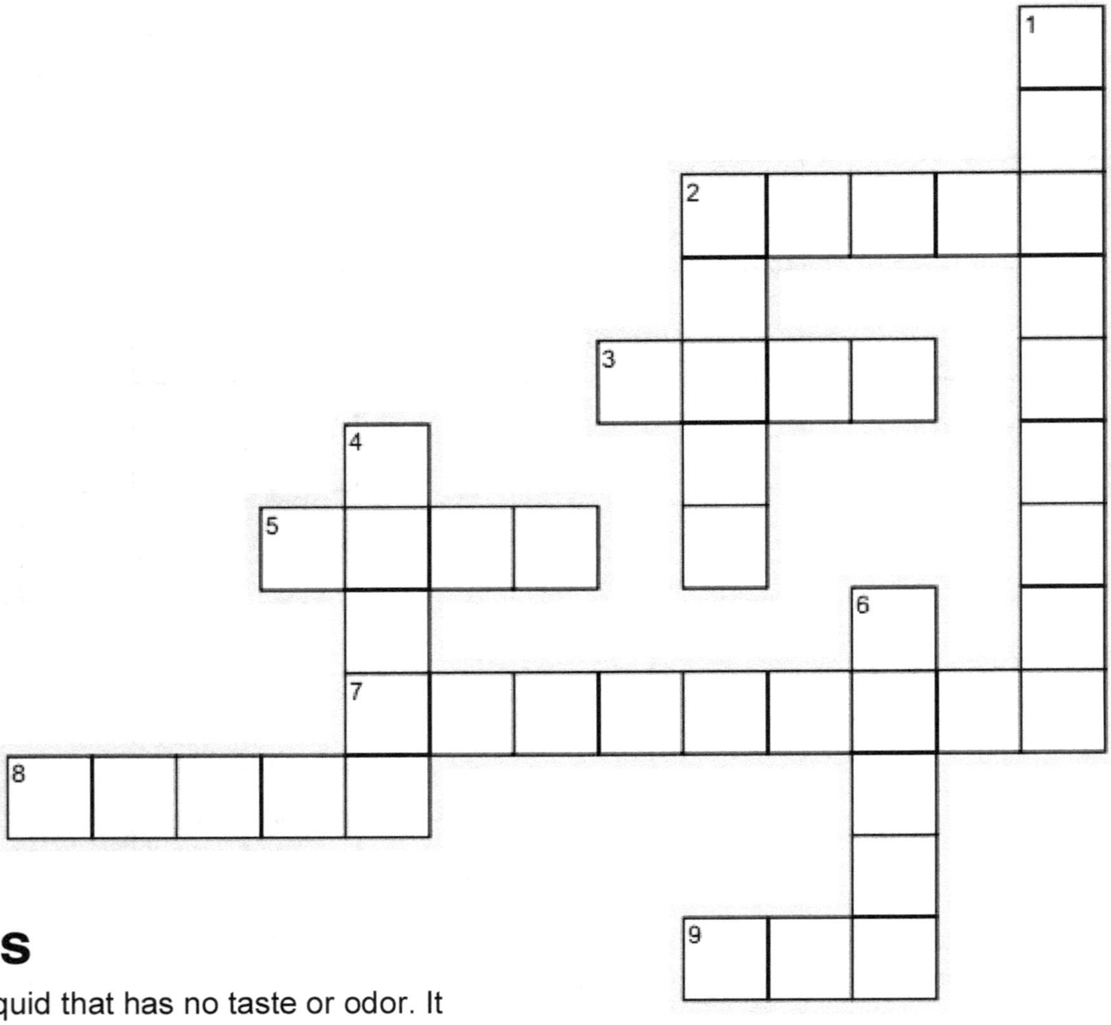

Across

2. A clear liquid that has no taste or odor. It takes the form of rain, rivers, oceans, and lakes and is a requirement for most forms of life.
3. A moving ridge or swell on the surface of a body of water.
5. A large vessel built to carry people or goods long distances through deep water.
7. A person hired to watch over a swimming area and rescue anyone who might be drowning.
8. A piece or length of soft cloth or paper used to wipe or dry the face, body, dishes, or other things.
9. Soaked, made moist, or covered with water or another liquid.

Down

1. A long, narrow board on which a person kneels, stands, or lies while riding the waves.
2. A structure built along a shore, and often into the water, where boats and ships dock; pier.
4. A hard outer covering of certain animals, such clams, snails, or oysters.
6. A small ship used for private trips or racing.

BIRTHDAY

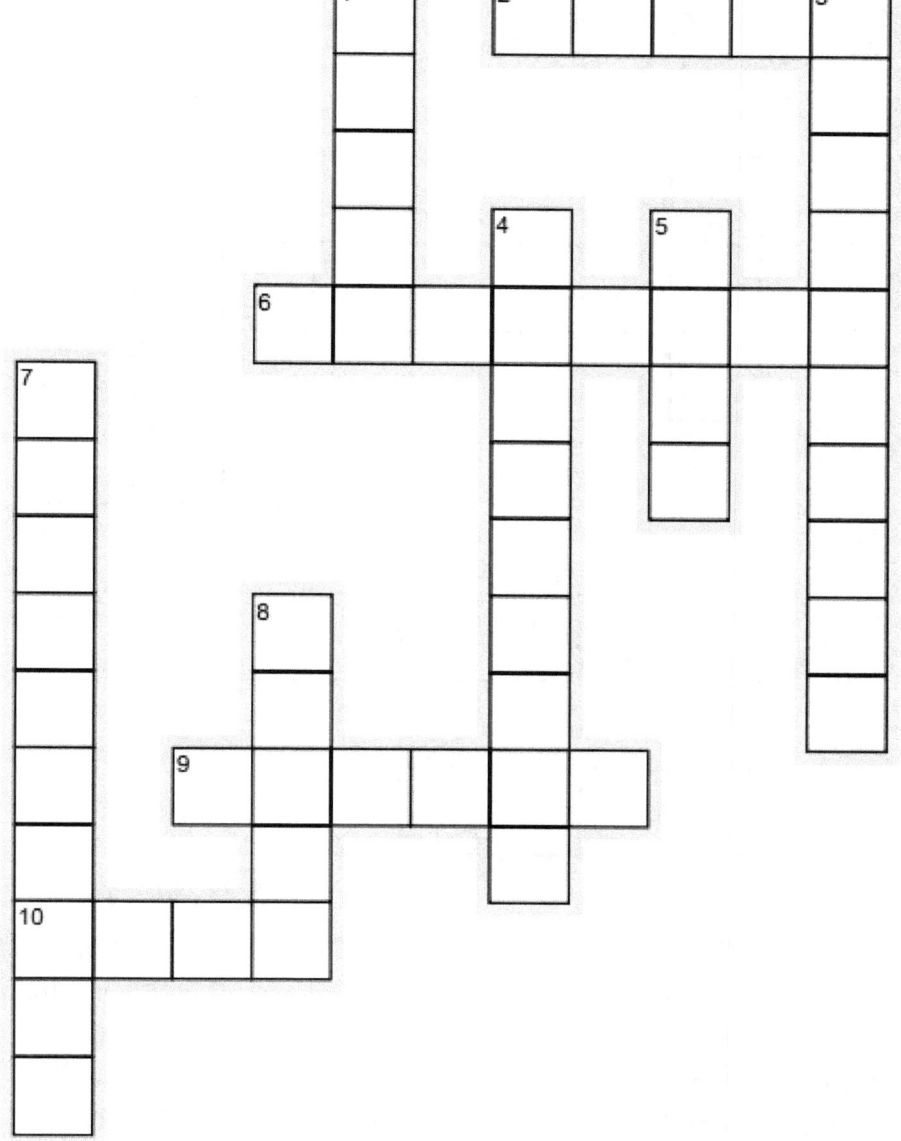

Across

2. Made of dough that is covered with tomato sauce and cheese; it is baked in an oven.
6. To make something look nice and pretty.
9. Children break it with a bat at a party in order to get the candy and toys.
10. Objects that children play with, for example a doll or a model car.

Down

1. Pressed from fruit or vegetables.
3. To like or enjoy an object or event.
4. A gathering of people in a special area.
5. A cooked sweet food using eggs, flour and fat, which is sometimes decorated with icing sugar.
7. Small sweets covered in a firm brown paste and grouped into a box.
8. Potatoes cooked and finely sliced with various flavours added.

BODY

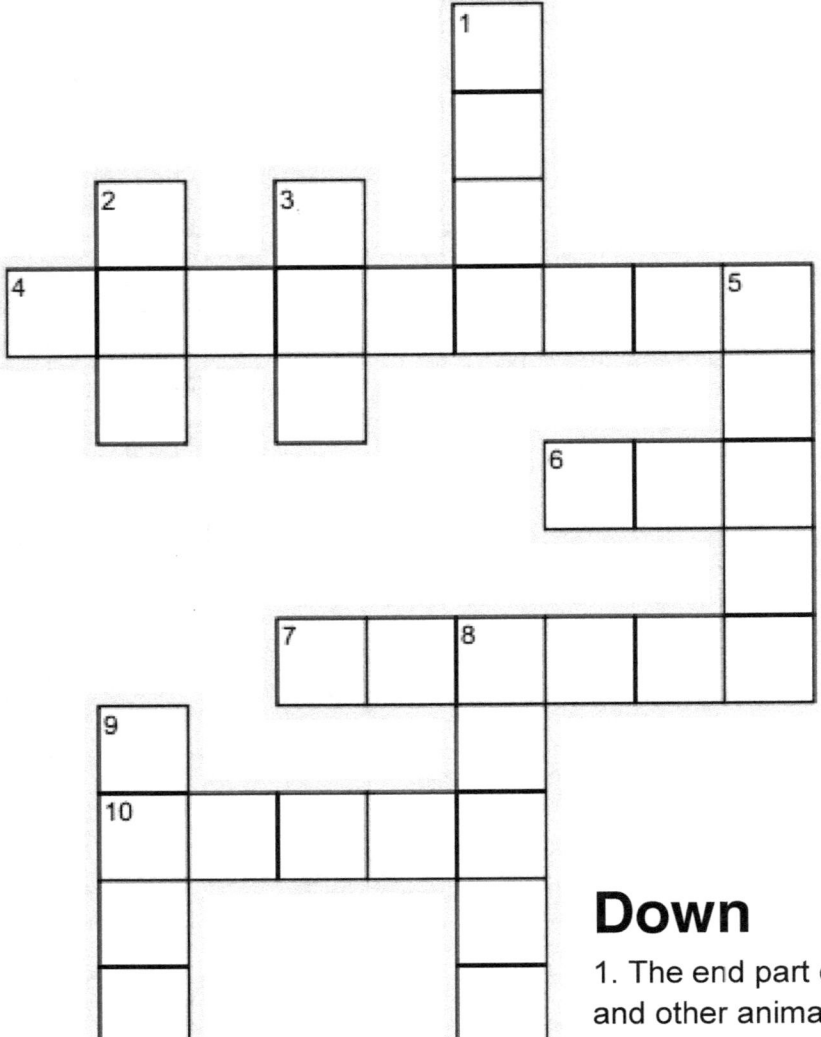

Across

4. The process by which the stomach and intestines change food into a form that the body can use as energy.

6. The organ of hearing in people and some other animals.

7. Tissue in the body of animals and humans that moves parts of the body. It is made up of bundles of fibers that move the body by tightening and relaxing.

10. The joint between the leg and the foot; the part of the leg just above the foot.

Down

1. The end part of the leg of humans and other animals, on which the body stands and walks.

2. The part on either side of the body between the waist and the thigh.

3. One of the body parts of an animal or human that is used for standing and walking.

5. Any of the fibers that carry messages to and from the brain and other parts of the body. They are bundled together into a complicated system that connects all parts of the body to the spinal cord and brain.

8. To give off a salty fluid from the skin pores to cool the body.

9. The part on the end of the human arm. It is used for grasping or holding.

CLASSROOM

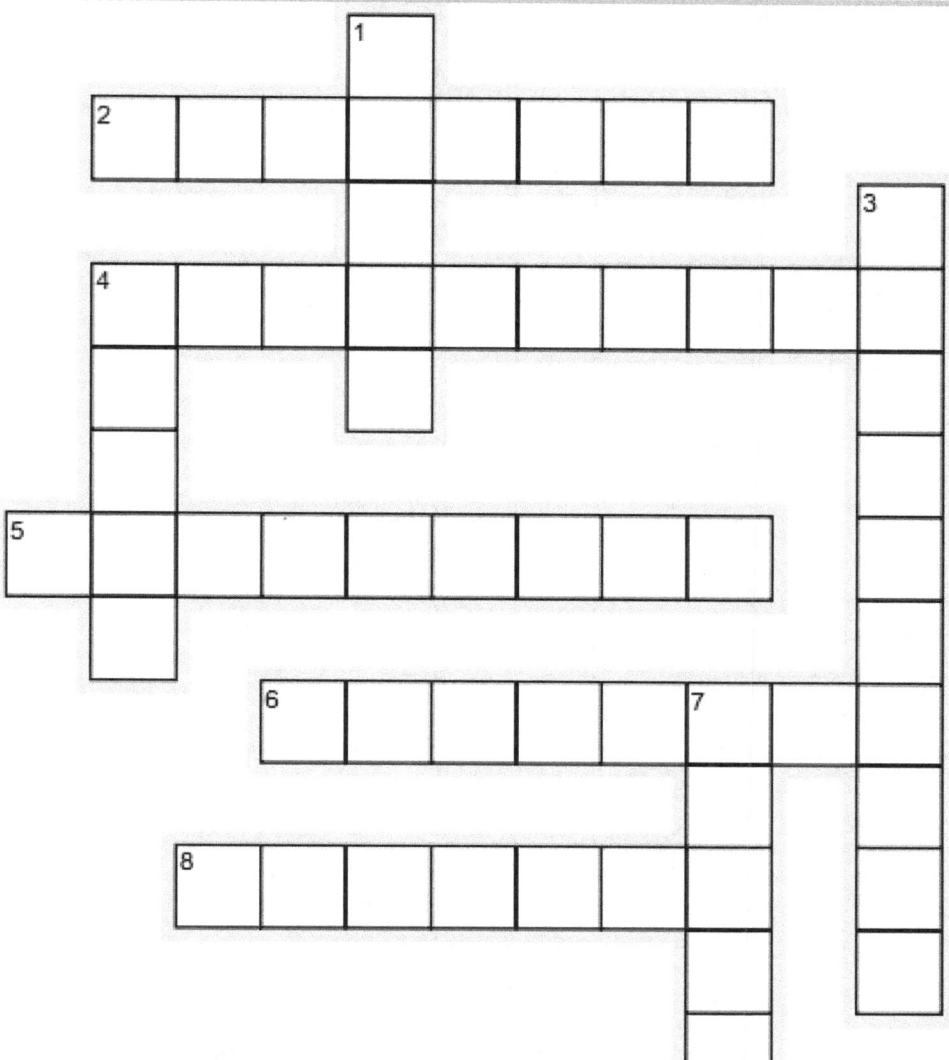

Across

2. An announcement or report of the latest events or things of current interest.
4. A machine or computer application used in calculating or computing numbers.
5. A small board with a spring clip at the top for holding papers, used as a portable writing surface.
6. A set of shelves for holding books.
8. An instrument for showing direction. It has a moving magnetic needle that points north.
9. A piece of furniture for one person to sit on. It has four legs, a back, and sometimes arms.

Down

1. A device, other than a watch, for measuring and showing the time.
3. The method and process of using whole numbers to add, subtract, multiply, and divide.
4. A piece of calcite or a similar substance, usually in the shape of a crayon, that is used to write or draw on blackboards or other flat surfaces.
7. The solution to a problem.

HALLOWEEN

Across

1. An actor who wears odd clothes and makeup to make people laugh. They act out jokes and do tricks in circuses, at parties, and at other events.
2. To form or write by cutting.
5. Feeling fear.
7. Any animal other than a human, especially a mammal with four legs.
8. The color of the night sky; the darkest color.
9. Causing alarm or fright.

Down

1. A place where the dead are buried; graveyard.
3. A small mammal that flies. They have small bodies and large wings covered with skin. Most of them eat at night, when they use sound to find and catch flying insects.
4. Strikingly odd or unusual, esp. in appearance or behavior.
6. A living being from another planet; extraterrestrial. There is no evidence that aliens exist, but many people believe there is life on other planets.

MATH

Across

2. Opposite or reversed in position, order, direction, nature, or effect.
5. A part or very small part of a whole.
7. The act or process of adding.
9. A solid figure with a shape similar to that of a can, a round flat cake, or a round tube with closed ends. It has parallel circular faces joined by one curved face.
10. The figure made by two lines or rays coming from a single point.

Down

1. The basic unit of length of the metric system, equal to one hundred centimeters or 3.28 feet.
3. The word for the Roman numeral XI.
4. A positive or negative whole number or zero.
6. Of a two-dimensional figure with straight sides, having two equal sides.
8. A solid figure with a flat base in the shape of a circle and one curved face that narrows into a point.

SPORTS

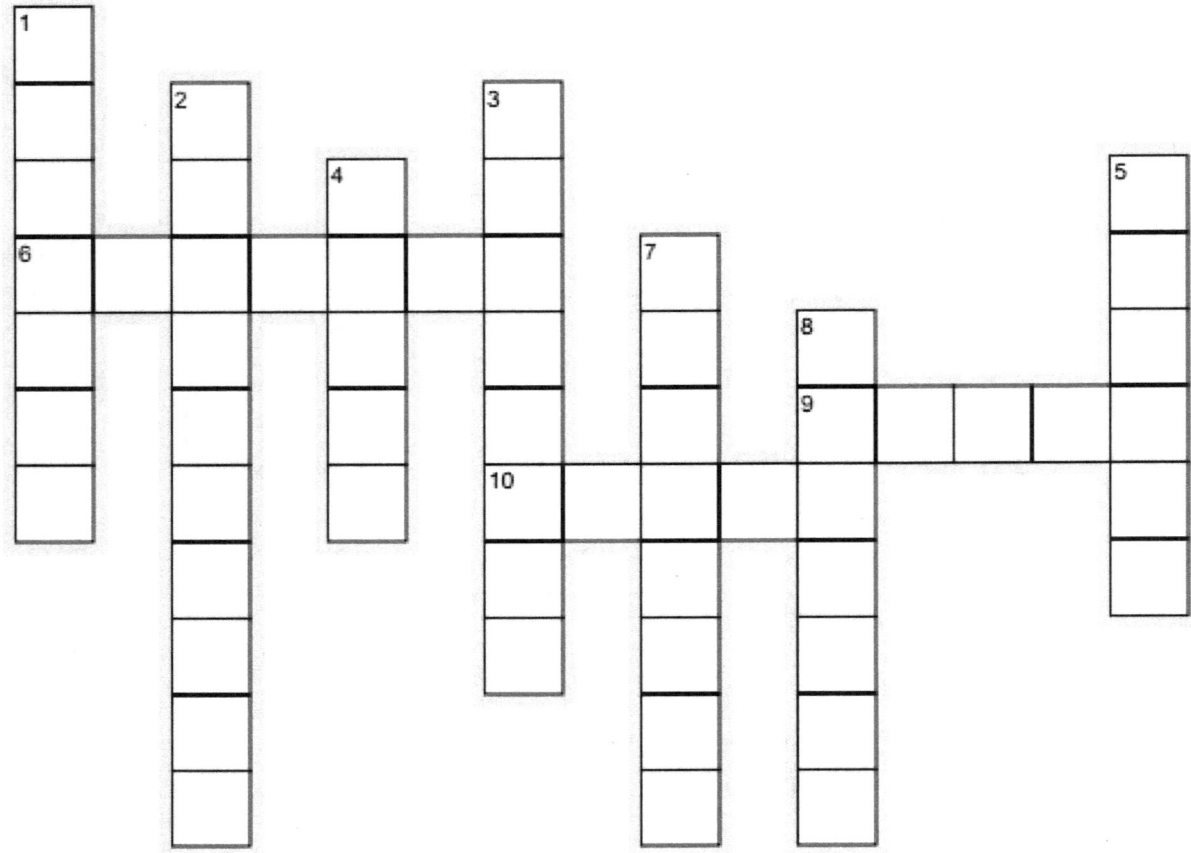

Across

6. Someone who is unqualified or not skilful enough.
9. _____ and field - a set of athletic events that take place on or near a running track. The events include running, jumping, and throwing.
10. A stage, ring, or other enclosed area where shows or sports events are held.

Down

1. A punishment given for breaking a law, rule, or agreement.
2. The player who defends the team's goal in sports such as soccer or hockey.
3. Of a stroke in tennis or the like, performed with the palm facing forward.
4. (Court game) put the ball into play
5. _____ room - a room containing lockers for storing clothes and equipment and often used for changing clothes, as at a gymnasium or pool.
7. A person or team that is expected to lose a contest in sports or politics.
8. A place used for sports events and other outdoor activities, which has rows of seats that rise up around an open field.

VERB

Across

1. To look closely or carefully.
5. If you _____ a fact or a situation, you accept or admit that it is true or that it exists.(FORMAL)
7. To move back and forth or up and down with quick motions.
8. To look at.
9. To show or help to gain knowledge.

Down

2. To prepare for eating by using heat.
3. To provide food for or give food to.
4. To move the feet and body in a rhythmic way, usually to music.
6. To no longer have; be unable to find; misplace.
8. To hit, wound, destroy, or kill with a bullet, arrow, or similar object.

ADJECTIVES

Across

1. Having greater than usual length in distance or time.
4. Full of activity, spirit, or excitement.
6. Having a low price.
7. Little in size, number, or amount.
8. Having lived for many years; not young.

Down

2. Having qualities that are desired.
3. Of, concerning, or consisting of an angel or angels; Marked by utter benignity; resembling or befitting an angel or saint
5. Having to do with sports and other physical activities; Relating to or befitting athletics or athletes.
7. Having little length; not long.
9. Having great space below or behind a certain point; reaching far down or back; not shallow.

AIR TRAVEL

Across

2. The operator of an Aircraft.
4. A device used to make an airplane or ship move forward. It is made of tilted blades that are attached to and spin around a hub.
5. The area from which the pilot and crew control an airplane.
8. Travel slowly
10. Suitcases, bags, or trunks used to carry things during travel; luggage.

Down

1. Get on _____ of (trains, buses, ships, aircraft, etc.)
3. The act of reaching a certain place or goal.
6. _____ flight - A flight with an intermediate stop and a change of aircraft (possibly a change of airlines)
7. A vehicle carrying many passengers; used for public transport.
9. The act or process, or an instance, of leaving the ground or other surface, as in preparation for flight.

ANIMALS

Across

2. A mammal with a very long neck, long legs, and hooves. They have short horns covered with fur.

4. A very large, round mammal that has short legs with hooves and thick skin with almost no hair. They live in or near rivers and lakes of tropical Africa. They eat plants.

5. A large, wild cat of Africa and southern Asia that has solid black spots on its fur. They have long legs and are the fastest animal on land. Sometimes they are trained for hunting game.

7. A young dog.

8. A very small mammal with a round body, short tail, and large pouches in its cheeks. They are rodents that live in burrows and come out at night to find food. They are often kept as pets or used in scientific experiments

9. An animal with a hard, jointed shell that lives in the ocean. They have four pairs of legs and a pair of large claws. They are a kind of crustacean.

Down

1. Bottom-living cephalopod having a soft oval body with eight long tentacles

2. A small fish that lives in fresh water. They are usually yellow or orange and are often kept in ponds or aquariums.

3. Any of various tailless stout-bodied amphibians with long hind limbs for leaping; semiaquatic and terrestrial species

6. A very large animal with a long, flexible nose called a trunk, which it uses to pick up things.

ANTONYMS

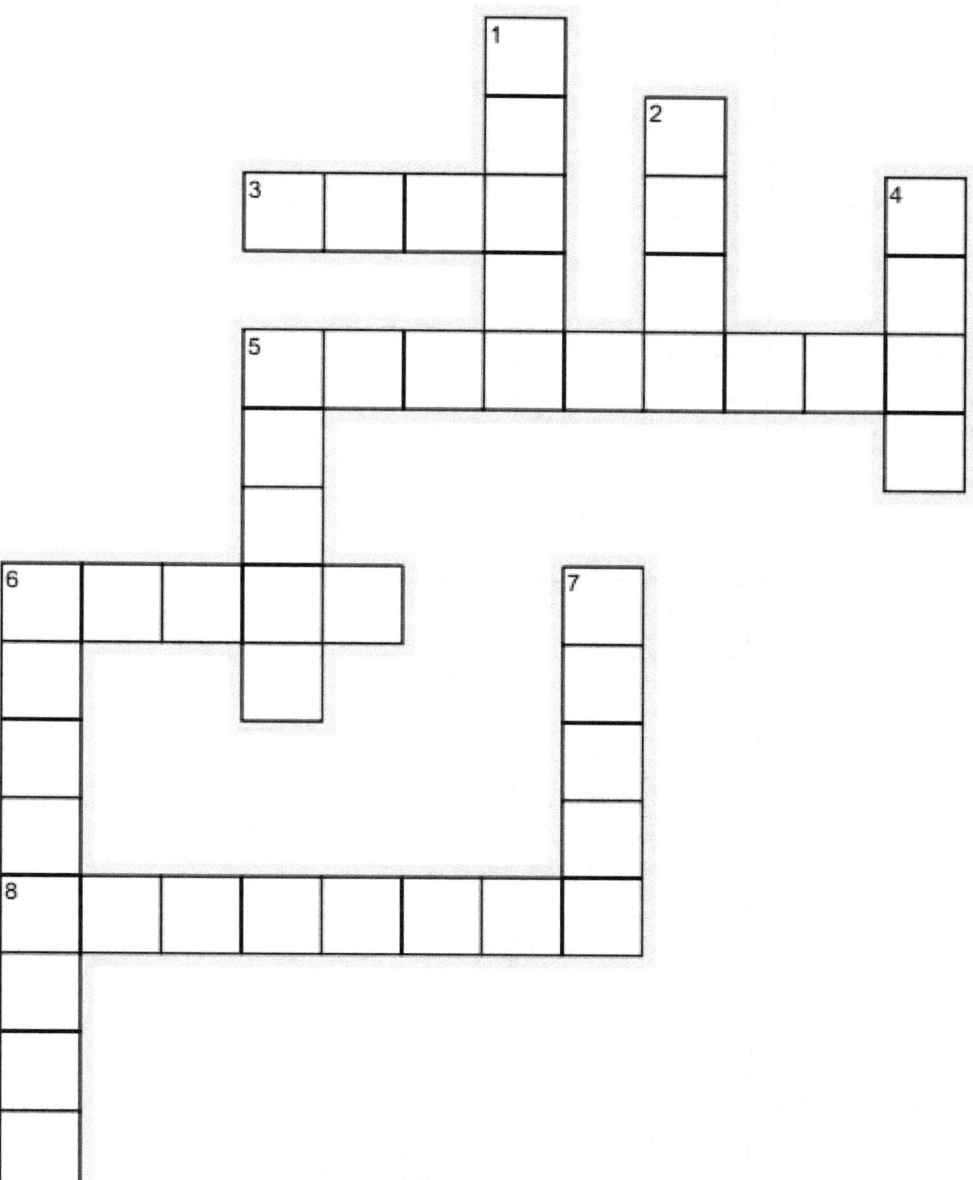

Across

3. Opposite of the word "far".
5. Opposite of the word "daytime".
6. Opposite of the word "inner".
8. Opposite of the word "majority".

Down

1. Opposite of the word "south".
2. Opposite of the word "messy".
4. Opposite of the word "under".
5. Opposite of the word "always".
6. Opposite of the word "pessimist".
7. Opposite of the word "quiet".

Across

2. An odd personal trait; idiosyncrasy.
4. To hold the interest of in a pleasant way; entertain.
5. _____ joke - A trick or prank played on someone.
8. Silly; foolish; not true.
9. Words or actions that have no meaning or make no sense.
10. A short story, usually with a funny ending, that is told to make people laugh.

Down

1. Cheerful or gay; carefree.
3. Believing almost anything; easily tricked.
6. Someone hired to tell jokes in royal courts during the Middle Ages in Europe. They often made fun of court life.
7. Causing laughter or amusement.

ASTRONOMY

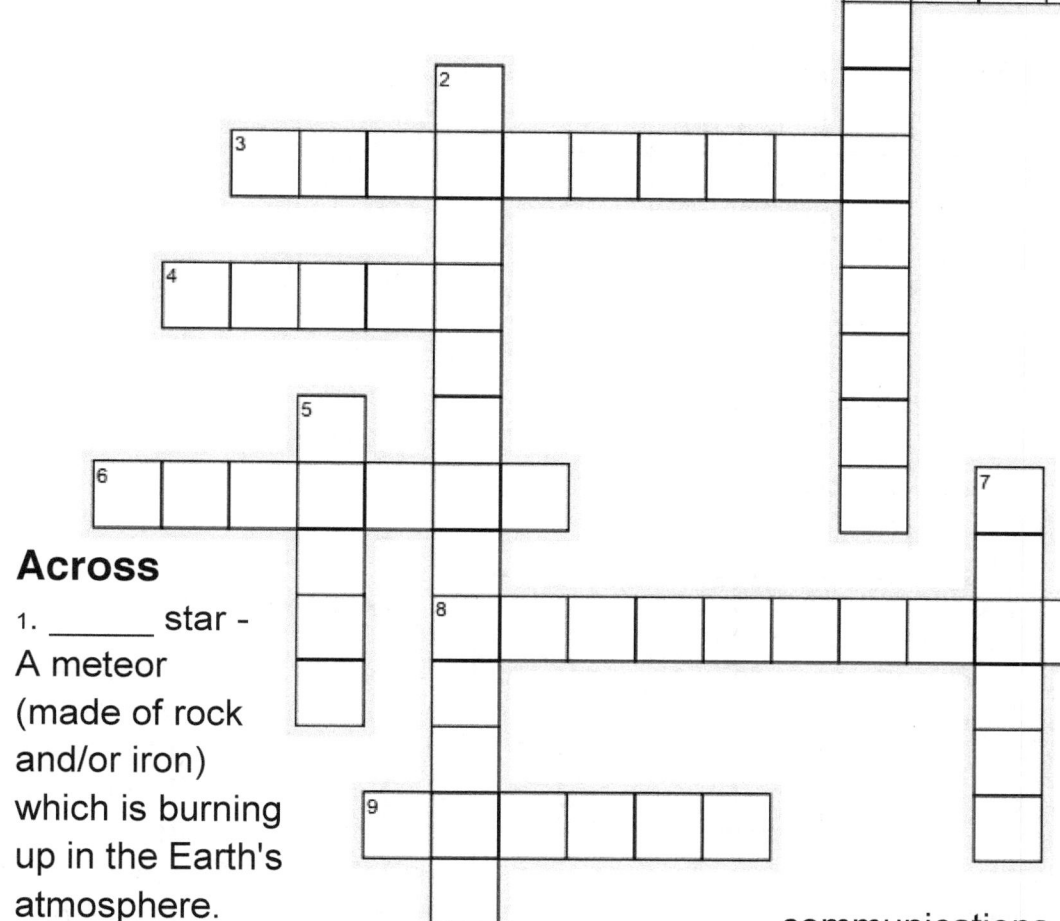

Across

1. _____ star - A meteor (made of rock and/or iron) which is burning up in the Earth's atmosphere.

3. The gas that surrounds a planet.

4. The second planet from the Sun.

6. Space _____ - It flies into space and back down again, carrying people and equipment.

8. They go up into space to explore.

9. A band of 12 constellations (groups of stars) in the sky, including Capricorn, Aquarius, Sagittarius, Scorpio, Libra, Virgo, Leo, Cancer, Gemini, Taurus, Aries, and Pisces.

Down

1. An object which has been sent into space in order to collect information or to be part of a communications system.

2. A group of stars that we see in the sky. They are not necessarily located together in space, but looks as though they are from Earth.

5. We see in the night sky is another sun, but much farther away than our sun.

7. A meteoroid that has entered the Earth's atmosphere, usually making a fiery trail as it falls; a shooting star. Most burn up before hitting the Earth.

BODY

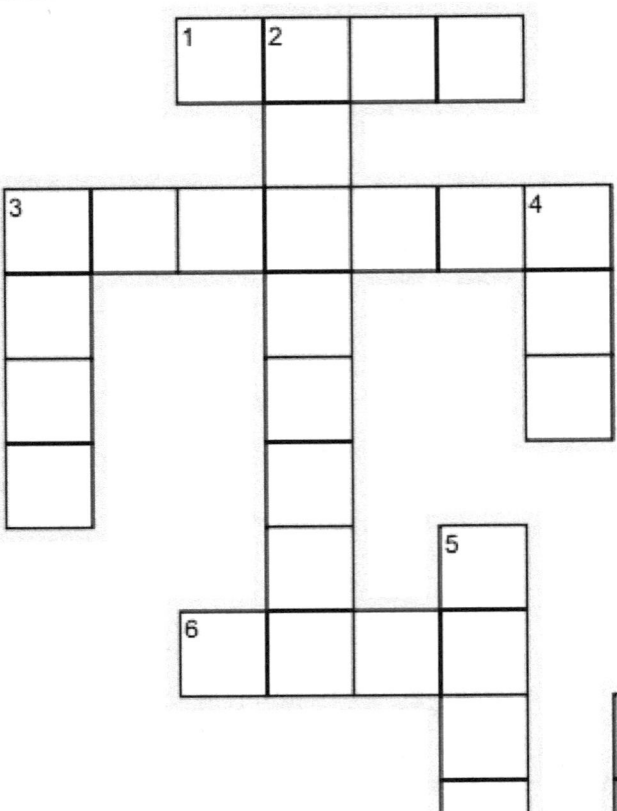

Down

2. Activity done to keep the body or mind strong or to make them stronger.
3. A substance used to cure or heal; medicine.
4. The organ of the body that gives animals sight, and the area close around it.
5. The organ inside the skull of humans and animals. It is the main part of the central nervous system. It controls the body's movements and activities, and is the center of thought, memory, and feelings.
7. The opening in the face through which one eats, breathes, and makes sounds.

Across

1. A tiny unit of plant or animal life, having a nucleus and surrounded by a very thin membrane.
3. A condition that causes harm to the health of a person, animal, or plant; illness; sickness.
6. A drop of salty liquid that comes from the eye. They clean the eye and keep it wet.
8. Any damage or wrong that causes pain or difficulty.
9. The part of the face below the mouth and above the neck; the center of the lower jaw.

BUILDING

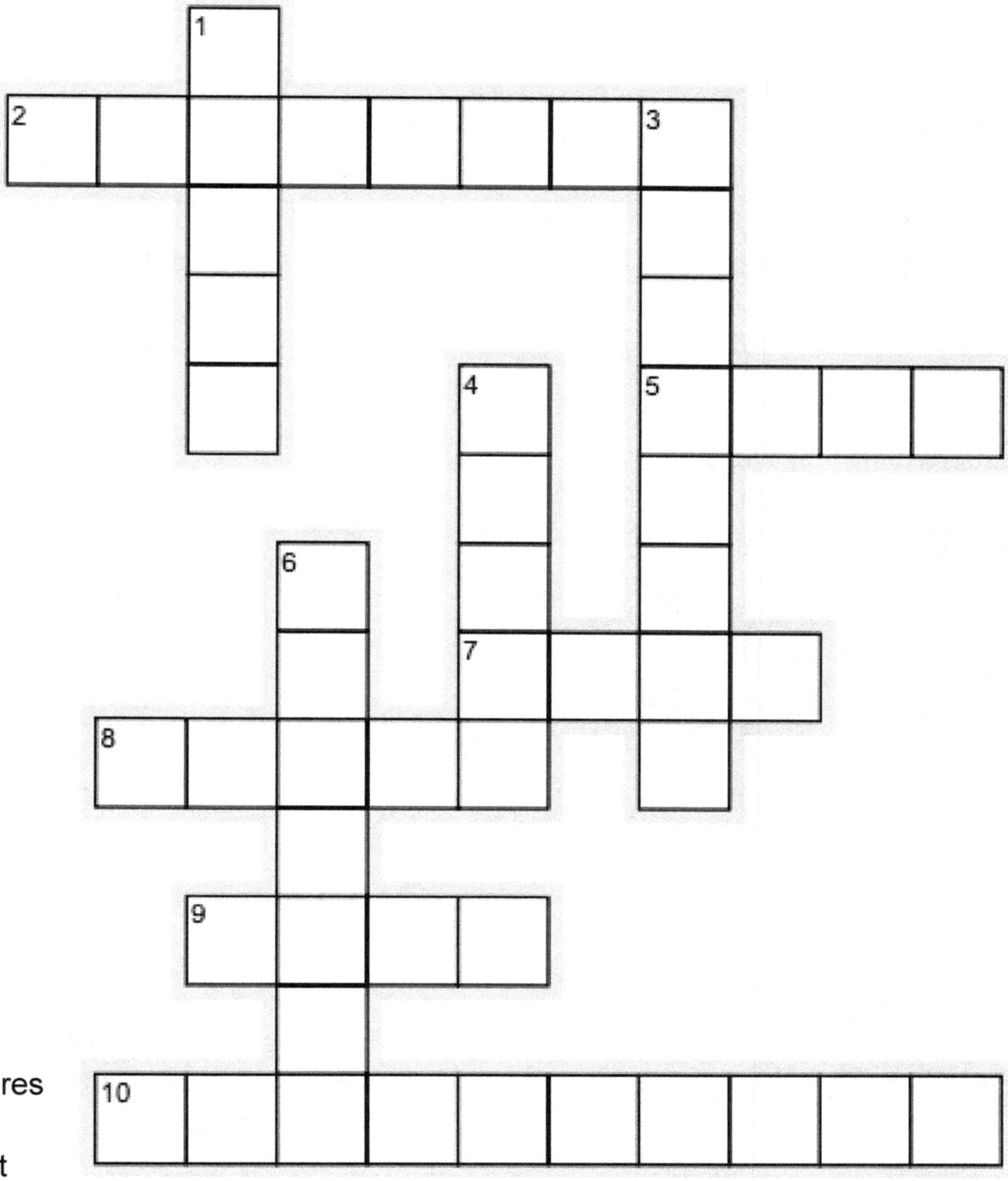

Across

2. Stone sculptures of grotesque creatures that sit perched atop some buildings; they act as waterspouts.
5. The top covering of a building.
7. A structure that is curved at the top and is supported on either side by a pillar, post, or wall.
8. Log _____ - a house made of logs.
9. You can put your money in a bank for safe keeping.
10. A very tall building.

Down

1. Rectangular blocks of baked clay used for building walls, which are usually red or brown.
3. The _____ to a place is the way into it, for example a door or gate.
4. Relating to or located in a city.
6. Has books, tapes, and computer programs.

CLASSROOM

Across

3. A thick, sticky liquid used to join things together.

4. A smooth, dark board to be written on with chalk; blackboard.

7. (Informal) a short form of gymnasium.

8. _____ paper - Heavy colored paper, used esp. by school children for drawing, crafts, and the like.

9. To get to know or gain knowledge of through study or experience.

Down

1. The world; planet Earth.

2. A colored stick or pencil made of wax. A crayon i s used for drawing and coloring.

4. An electronic device that is used to store and sort information and work with data at a high speed.

5. A book, or a source of information found on a computer, that lists the words of a language in alphabetical order, along with information about their meaning, spelling, and pronunciation.

6. A meal eaten in the middle of the day, or any light meal during the day.

HALLOWEEN

Across

2. Causing great fear or terror.
3. _____-pocus - Meaningless or nonsensical words or phrases repeated by magicians.
5. The title character of Mary W. Shelley's early nineteenth-century novel, who creates a monster that destroys him.
7. Mysterious control of physical forces or events through spells or special ceremonies.
8. An imaginary tiny creature in human form, thought to have magic powers.
9. A case or container that is made of a material through which a light can shine and be protected.

Down

1. The spirit of a person who has died, especially one that is believed to haunt a place or living people.
3. Causing a feeling of fear, horror; dreadful.
4. Stern or harsh.
6. An imaginary small creature that looks like a human and has magical powers.

HOME

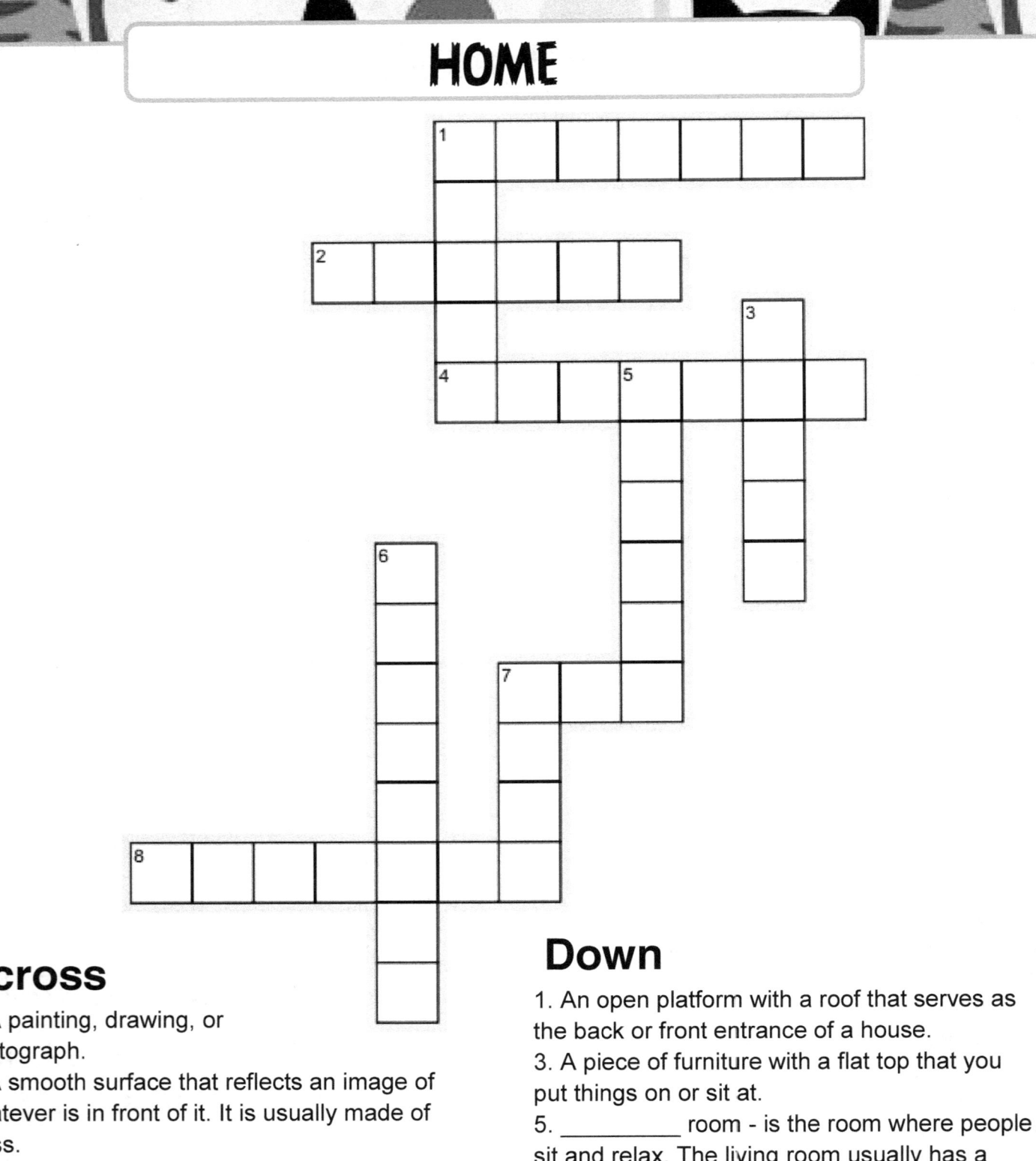

Across

1. A painting, drawing, or photograph.
2. A smooth surface that reflects an image of whatever is in front of it. It is usually made of glass.
4. A long narrow passage with doors into rooms on both sides of it.
7. A piece of thick material used to cover part of a floor.
8. A room used for sleeping in.

Down

1. An open platform with a roof that serves as the back or front entrance of a house.
3. A piece of furniture with a flat top that you put things on or sit at.
5. _____ room - is the room where people sit and relax. The living room usually has a couch and comfortable chairs.
6. A room in a house that contains a bath or shower, a washbasin, and sometimes a toilet.
7. Space that is used or available for use.

INSECT

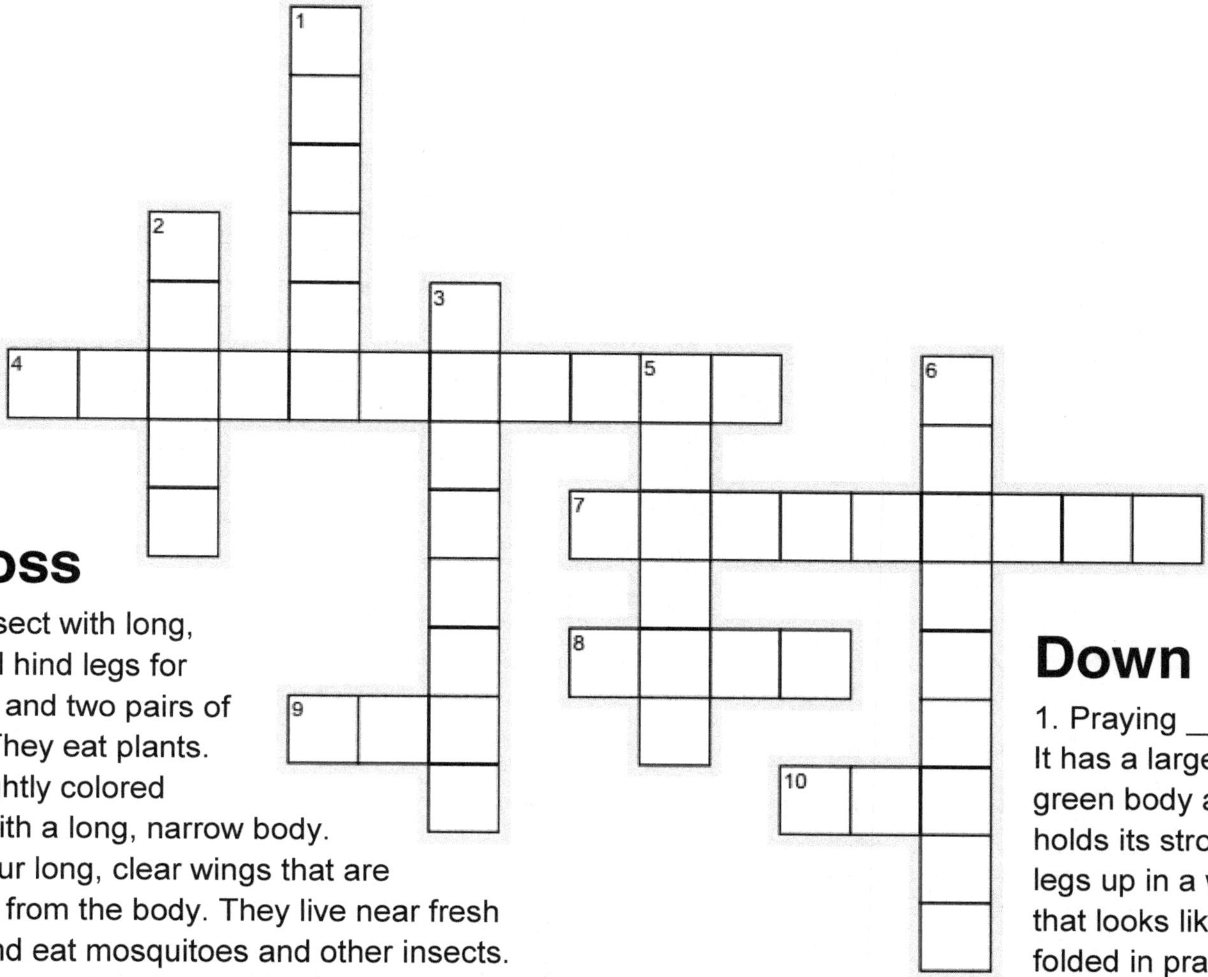

Across

4. An insect with long, powerful hind legs for jumping and two pairs of wings. They eat plants.

7. A brightly colored insect with a long, narrow body. It has four long, clear wings that are held out from the body. They live near fresh water and eat mosquitoes and other insects.

8. A small animal that is related to the spider. They attach themselves to people and other animals and suck their blood. They are known to spread disease.

9. An insect that lives in large, organized groups called colonies. Most of them live in or on the ground. They are related to bees and wasps.

10. An insect with a hairy body, four wings, and sometimes a stinger. Some of them live in social groups, and some live alone. Many of them drink nectar from flowers.

Down

1. Praying _____ - It has a large, bright green body and holds its strong front legs up in a way that looks like hands folded in prayer.

2. _____ widow - A small spider of North and South America. The female has a shiny, black body with a red mark on her underside and a poisonous bite.

3. An insect with a thin body and two wings. The females bite and suck the blood of animals and people. Some of them spread disease.

5. A nocturnal insect having a pincerslike structure at the rear of the abdomen.

6. A small animal with a narrow body like a worm. The front legs have poison claws. They are a kind of arthropod and are active at night.

Down

1. A place for teaching and learning.
2. A large school, where people both learn and do research. A student must finish high school first. They offer several levels of degrees.
4. An area of land, along with buildings and equipment, used to grow crops or raise animals for food or clothing.
6. A large and important town where many people live and work.
7. An area with streets, houses, and buildings that is larger than a village but usually smaller than a city.
9. An area of public land, as in a city, that is set aside for rest and enjoyment.

Across

3. Any location outside the Earth's atmosphere.
5. A place where books, records, and other materials are kept and from which they may be borrowed.
6. A large area of land where people live under the same government or have the same culture; nation.
8. A health facility where patients receive treatment.

MATERIAL

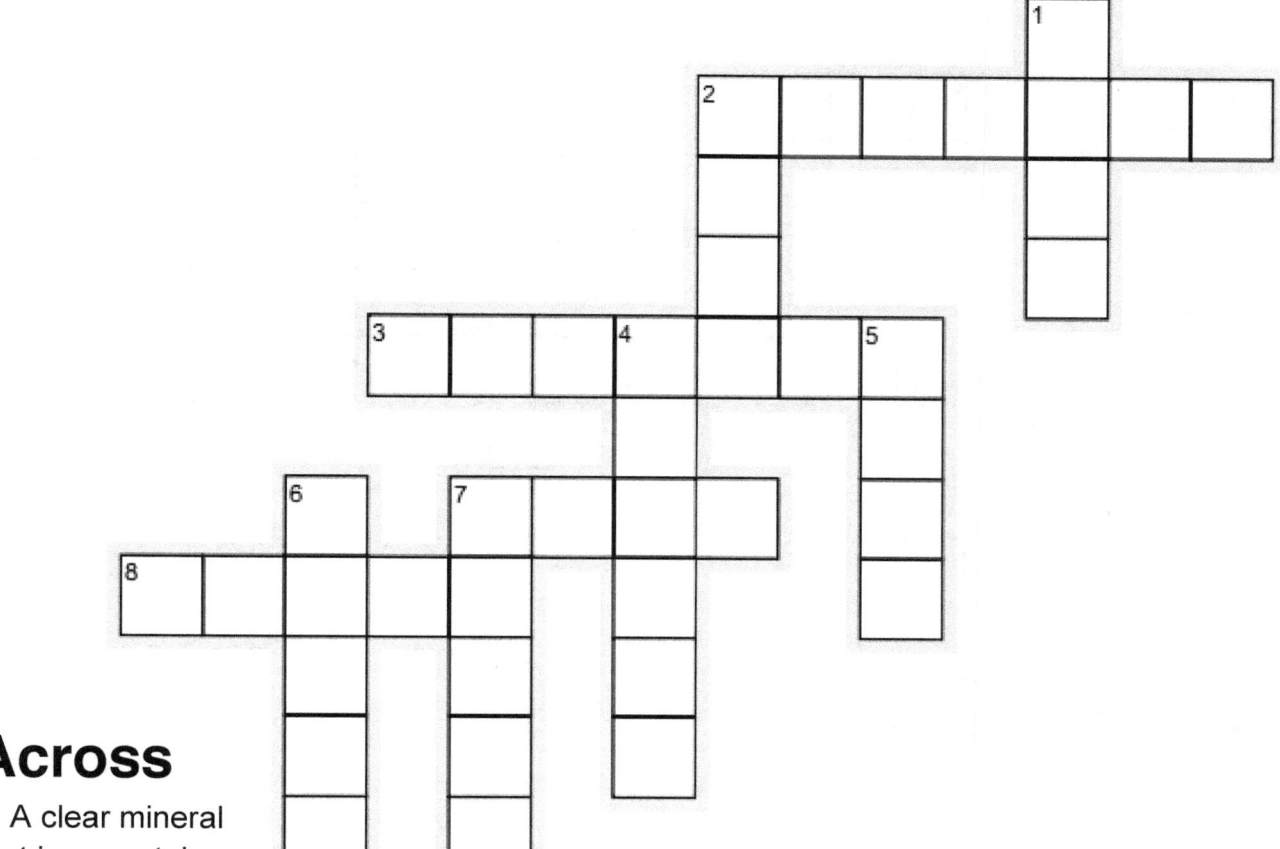

Across

2. A clear mineral that is a crystal form of pure carbon. They are the hardest natural substance known. They are used in making jewelry and as tools for cutting hard materials.

3. An artificial substance made from certain kinds of chemicals that can be easily shaped when soft. It is formed into many materials and products.

7. A soft, heavy, yellow metal that is one of the chemical elements. It is often combined with other metals to make it harder and stronger. It is very valuable.

8. Any solid mineral element that exhibits certain characteristics such as the ability to conduct heat or electricity. Most of them may be shaped under heat or pressure. Ex. Iron, silver, copper, and gold.

Down

1. The hard material lying under the bark that makes up the trunk and branches of a tree.

2. Tiny, dry pieces of soil, dirt, or other material.

4. A shiny white metal that is soft and easy to shape. It is one of the chemical elements. It is used in making jewelry, coins, and table utensils.

5. Moist, stiff earth that is used for making brick, pottery, and tile.

6. Hard matter formed from mineral and earth material; rock.

7. A hard, clear material that breaks easily. It is used to make windows, bottles, mirrors, and the like.

MATH

Across

4. Divisible by two.
6. The degree of heat or cold of an object or an environment.
8. A unit of weight equal to 16 ounces or 453.592 grams. (abbreviated: lb.)
9. A measure for arcs and angles.

Down

1. The quality of being heavy.
2. Based on the number ten.
3. One of two or more integers that can be exactly divided into another integer
4. A statement in arithmetic that uses an equal sign to show the equality of two quantities.
5. A group of symbols that make a mathematical statement.
7. The word for the Roman numeral IV.

SPORTS

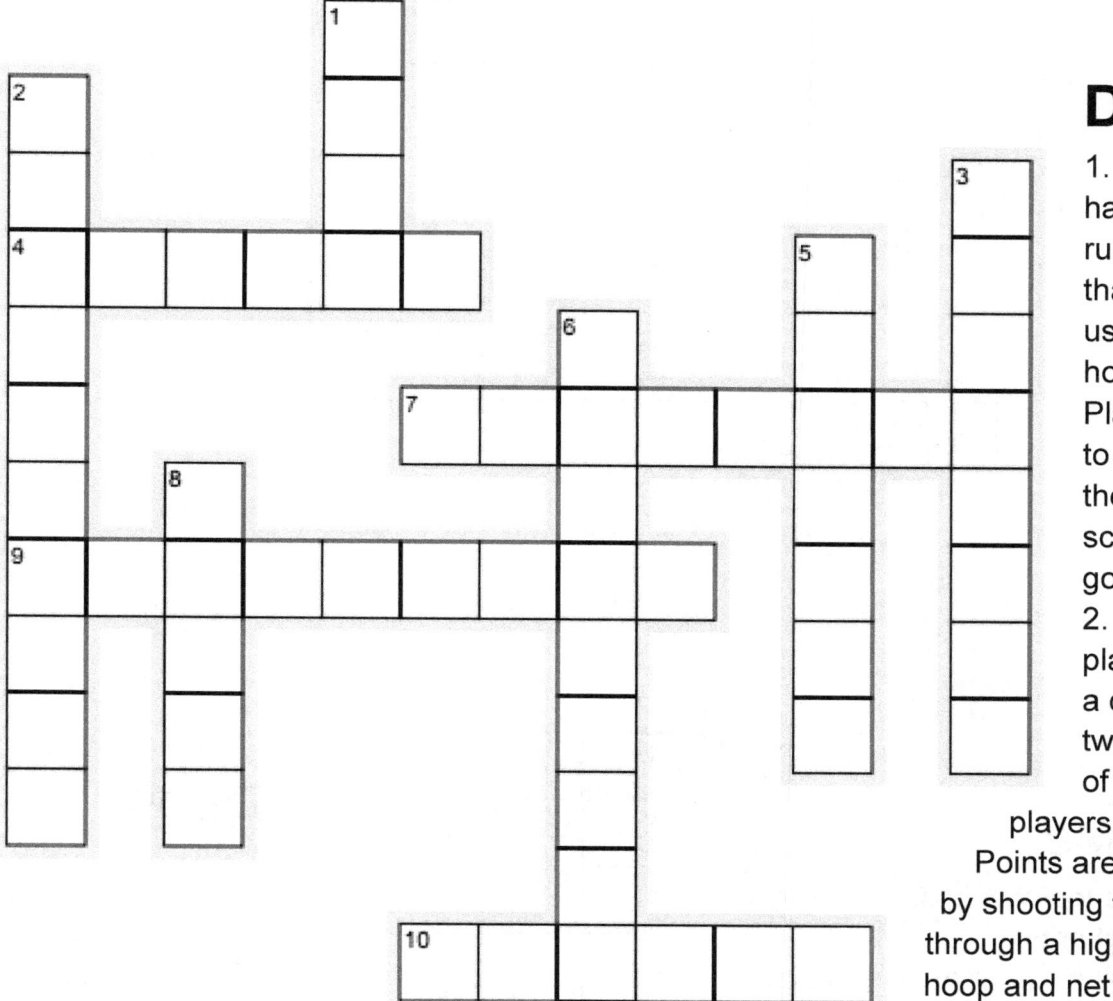

Down

1. The hard rubber disk that is used in ice hockey. Players try to hit it into the net to score a goal.
2. A game played on a court by two teams of five players each. Points are scored by shooting the ball through a high metal hoop and net at the opponent's end of the court.
3. Having to do with sports and other physical activities.
5. A large structure for open-air sports or entertainments.
6. A contest of skill including a series of games where those who lose one game may no longer take part.
8. The record of the total points earned in a game or test.

Across

4. To hit with the hand or a weapon.
7. A game played in the United States and Canada by two teams on a long field. Each team tries to score points by passing or carrying the ball to the other team's end of the playing area, or by kicking it through the goal posts.
9. The board to which a basketball hoop is attached.
10. The unit of a baseball of softball game during which each side has a turn at bat.

TOOLS

Across

1. A hand tool that is used to hold or twist a nut or bolt.
4. A metal tool with a sharp edge, used for cutting stone, wood, or metal.
5. A hand tool with a solid, heavy head on a handle. It is used to pound or to beat something into shape or place.
6. A slim, pointed metal rod with a flat top. It is hammered into pieces of wood or other material in order to fasten them together.
7. A toothed bar or wheel made to be engaged by a pawl so that motion is permitted in only one direction.
10. A tool that has a pair of jaws connected to handles and is used for holding, bending, or cutting things.

Down

2. Something that compresses, esp. a device for compressing and condensing gases to drive machinery.
3. A tool for turning a screw. It has a handle for turning and a long metal piece that fits the head of the screw.
8. A device used to fasten, support, or press together two or more objects or pieces.
9. trowel Any hand tool that has a flat blade. They are used to work with plaster and cement.

TRANSPORT

Across

3. _____ lounge - lounge where passengers can await departure
5. A place where aircraft land and take off, which has buildings and facilities for passengers.
8. A vehicle used to carry ill or injured people to a hospital.
9. _____ pass - An official card that you have to show before you get onto a plane
10. A vehicle with wings; and is driven by propellers or a jet engine.

Down

1. Caused to be slower or later.
2. Consists of the bags that you take with you when you travel.
4. A small, motorized vehicle designed for transportation on a golf course.
6. A document issued by a country to a citizen allowing that person to travel abroad and re-enter the home country
7. An instance of traveling by air

VALENTINE'S DAY

Across

1. A sweet food made of sugar and flavorings such as chocolate or peppermint.
7. A folded paper covering or container usually used to mail letters.
9. A spiritual being who acts as a servant or messenger of God. They are often represented as human figures with wings and a halo.
10. To have a high opinion of; respect.

Down

2. Strong affection or loyalty.
3. The part of a plant that has petals and that makes fruit or seeds; blossom. They often have a pleasant smell.
4. Words or actions used to greet others.
5. The condition or feeling of being infatuated.
6. An object of romantic love or infatuation.
8. The god of love in Roman mythology.

VERB

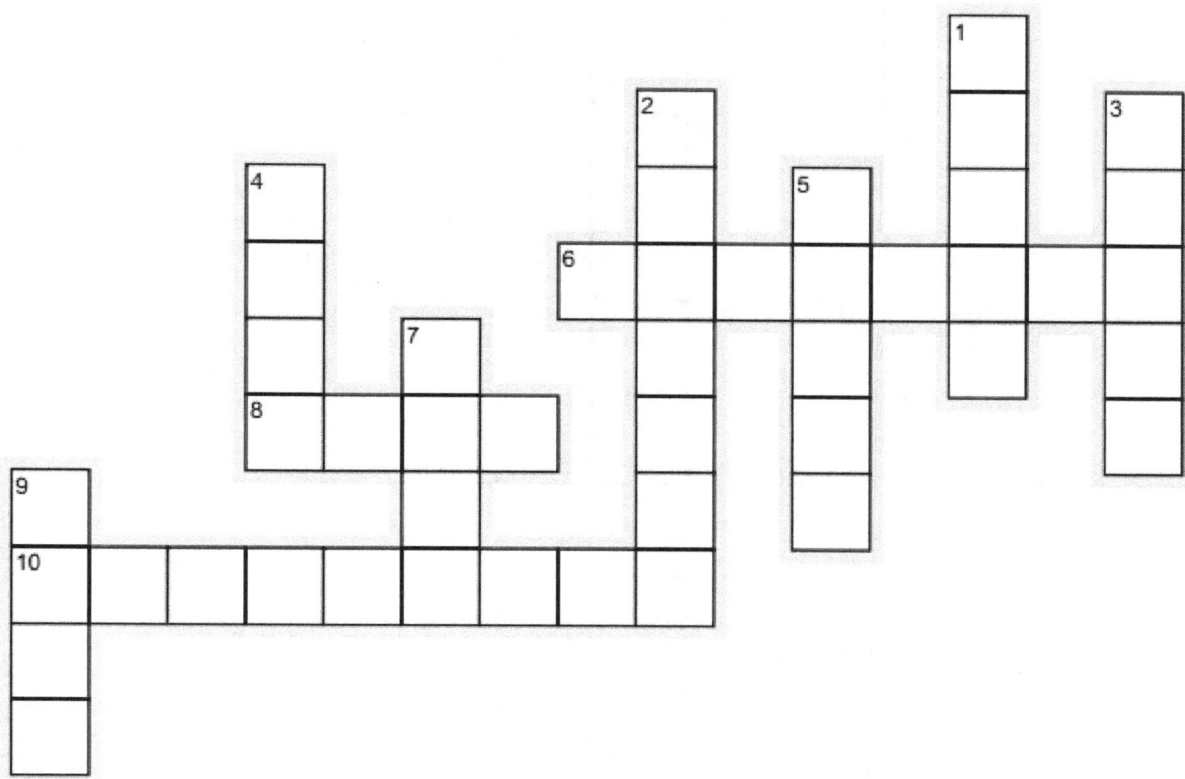

Across

6. You tell people about something publicly or officially.
8. To mix or move in a circle with a hand or object.
10. To make excuse for or regretful acknowledgment of a fault or offense.

Down

1. To list or name one by one in order to find the total.
2. (Medicine) dress by covering or binding
3. To sense the odor of by means of the nose.
4. To touch or press with the lips as a sign of love, friendship, passion, or respect.
5. To put one's hand or fingers on in order to feel.
7. To make musical sounds with the voice.
9. To say in a loud voice or shout out.

ADJECTIVES

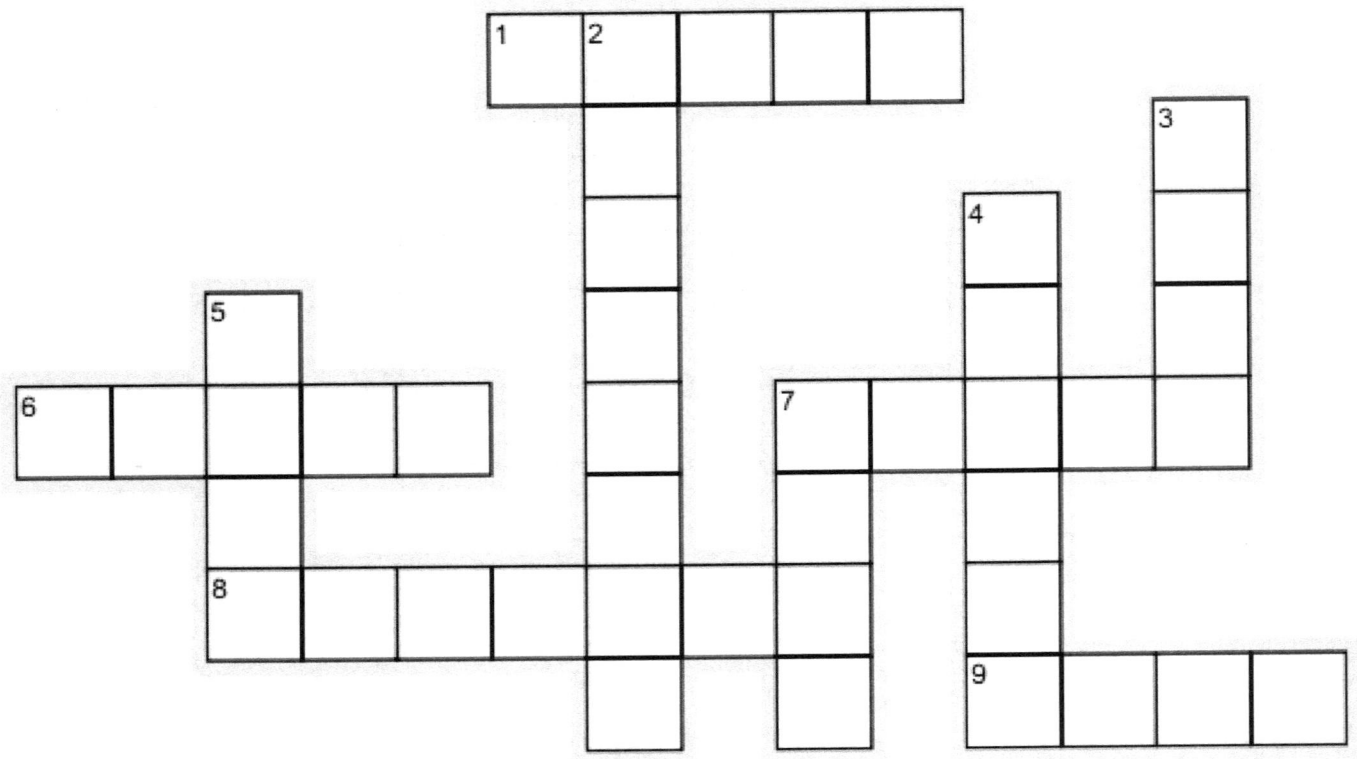

Across

1. Hanging in a loose way; puffed out.
6. Not dirty or stained.
7. Not clean; soiled.
8. Of, or having to do with, or being the nucleus of an atom or a cell.
9. No longer alive.

Down

2. Feeling strong affection for and not wanting to part with.
3. A very young girl or boy; infant.
4. Having the shape of a curve; not straight or angular.
5. Not nice; nasty or cruel.
7. Having little or no light.

ANTONYMS

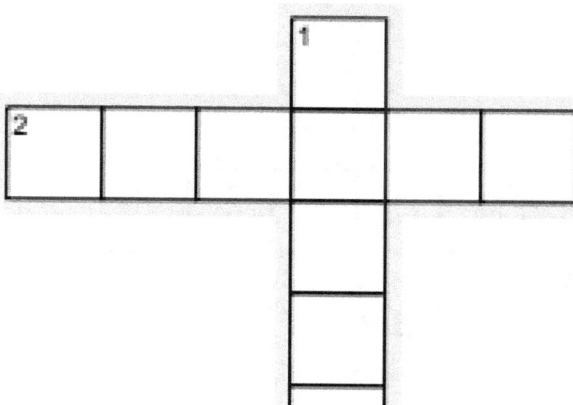

Across

2. Opposite of the word "immature".
3. Opposite of the word "minor".
4. Opposite of the word "tenant".
6. Opposite of the word "more".
7. Opposite of the word "dark".

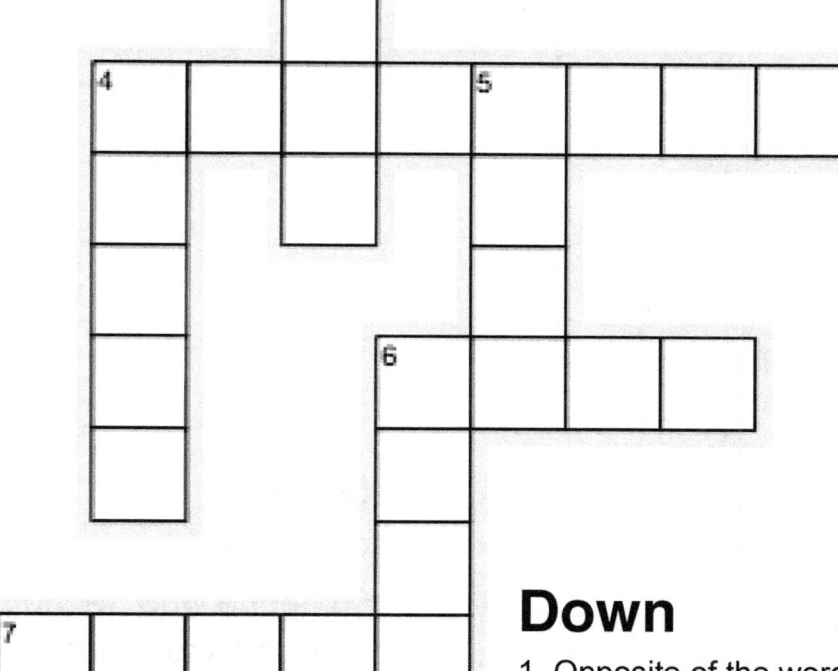

Down

1. Opposite of the word "senior".
3. Opposite of the word "few".
4. Opposite of the word "small".
5. Opposite of the word "dislike".
6. Opposite of the word "first".

APRIL FOOL'S DAY

Across

3. A quality that makes people laugh or feel amused.
6. (Informal) a joke or prank.
7. To cause to believe something that is not true; trick or fool.
8. A humorous imitation; good-natured mocking; lampoon.

Down

1. Funny; amusing.
2. Someone who frequently tells jokes or acts so as to provoke laughter; jokester.
3. An act meant to trick or deceive.
4. Silly; foolish; laughable.
5. Characterized by oddities or peculiarities.
9. A teasing trick; stunt.

ASTRONOMY

Across

1. People who study astronomy and learn about objects in the universe, like stars and planets.
3. The largest planet in our solar system and the fifth planet from the sun.
5. Is a building with a large telescope from which scientists study things such as the planets by watching them.
6. A medium-sized yellow star in our Solar System. We get our light and most of our energy from it.
9. It happens when the moon blocks out light from the sun or the Earth's shadow goes across the moon.
10. The smallest amount of a substance that can take part in a chemical reaction.

Down

2. The sixth planet from the Sun. It has beautiful rings.
4. _____ moon - smaller than a half moon.
7. Tiny stones or pieces of metal that travel through space.
8. _____ Way - bright line of stars stretching across the night sky.

BEACH

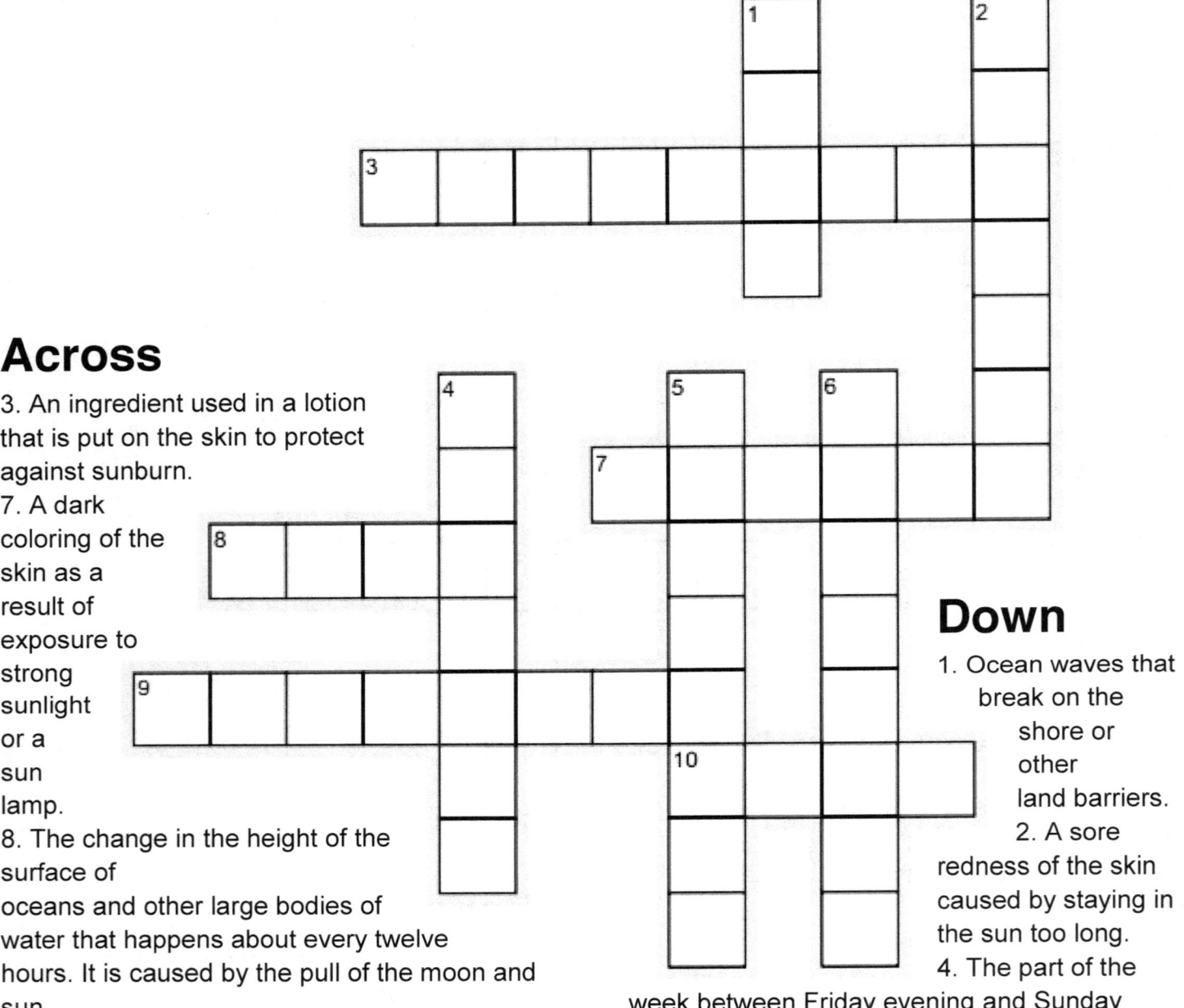

Across

3. An ingredient used in a lotion that is put on the skin to protect against sunburn.

7. A dark coloring of the skin as a result of exposure to strong sunlight or a sun lamp.

8. The change in the height of the surface of oceans and other large bodies of water that happens about every twelve hours. It is caused by the pull of the moon and sun.

9. A screen made of fabric stretched over a folding frame. It is used to shield against the rain or sun.

10. The act of traveling; a journey.

Down

1. Ocean waves that break on the shore or other land barriers.

2. A sore redness of the skin caused by staying in the sun too long.

4. The part of the week between Friday evening and Sunday evening.

5. To bare the body to the sun's rays.

6. A sea animal with a flat body and five or more arms. They are also called sea stars.

BIRTHDAY

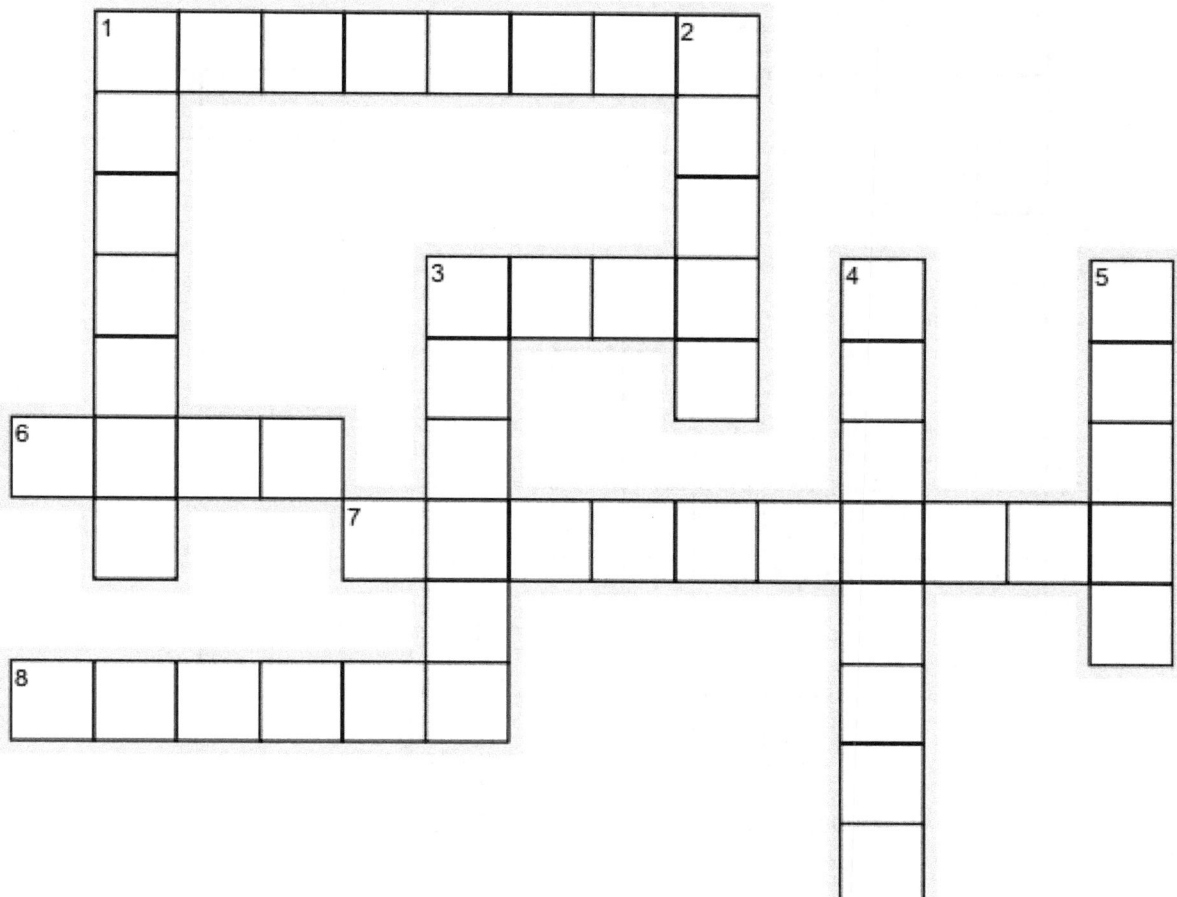

Across

1. Soft sugar mixed to a paste with liquid and spread on the top of cakes.
3. An appointment to meet someone, or the specific day that something happens.
6. Gift _____ - Same as wrapping paper.
7. A way of asking someone to come to a party.
8. The people who come to a party.

Down

1. The part of a plant which is often brightly colored, grows at the end of a stem, and only survives for a short time.
2. An activity that is done with a group of people for enjoyment.
3. Liquids to refresh a thirst.
4. Delighted, very thankful
5. Soft sugar mixed to a paste with liquid and spread on the top of cakes (same as frosting).

BODY

Across

1. The front part of the head from the forehead to the chin and from ear to ear.
2. In anatomy, the opening at the lower or rear end of the intestines, through which solid waste matter is excreted.
3. The part of the body between the chest and the hips. It contains the stomach, intestines, and liver.
4. A small muscular sac that is attached to the liver and that stores bile.
5. A tube that moves food from the mouth to the stomach of an animal.

Down

1. A hard, clear piece that grows at the end of the finger.
2. The joint between the leg and the foot; the part of the leg just above the foot.
3. Study of the structure of the bodies of people or animals.
5. The bend or joint between the upper arm and the lower arm.
6. First _____ - Emergency care given before regular medical aid can be obtained

BUILDING

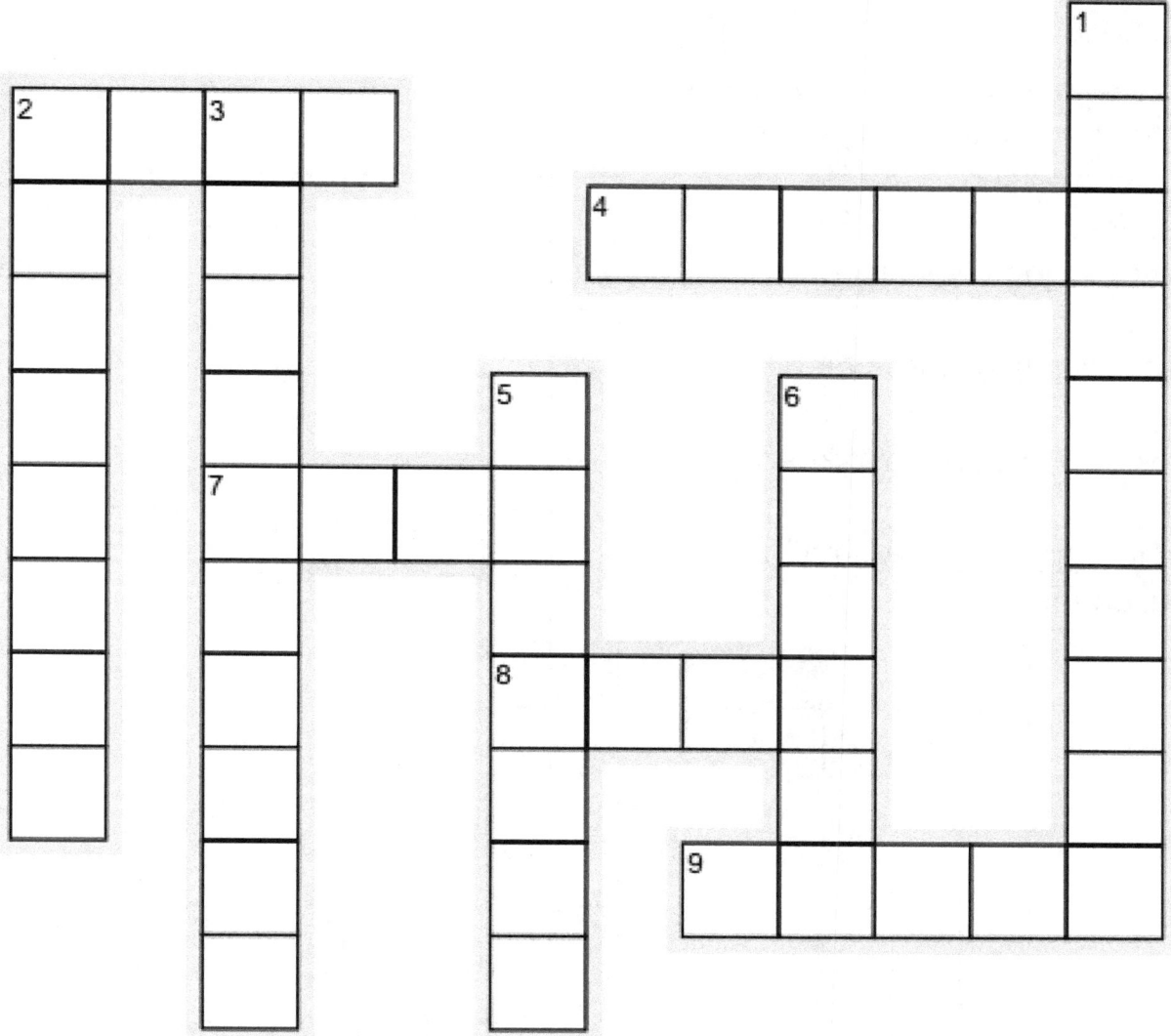

Across

2. A side of a building or a room or a fence.
4. A huge house where a king or queen lives.
7. A temporary shelter made of fabric.
8. A piece of wood, glass, or metal, which is moved to open and close the entrance to a building, room, cupboard, or vehicle.
9. _____ House - is where the President of the United States lives and works.

Down

1. A building, usually made out of glass, in which people grow plants.
2. It uses the wind to generate power.
3. Shines a very bright light so ships won't sail ashore or into rocks by mistake.
5. A large building in which sports events are held.
6. Is a building in which Christians worship.

CLASSROOM

Across

1. A tool in a home or office that uses staples to attach papers together.
3. A tool for measuring the length of something.
4. One whose job is teaching; instructor.
7. A measuring stick three feet long.
9. A book of blank pages to keep notes in.
10. pencil _____ - A small device used for making pencils sharp.

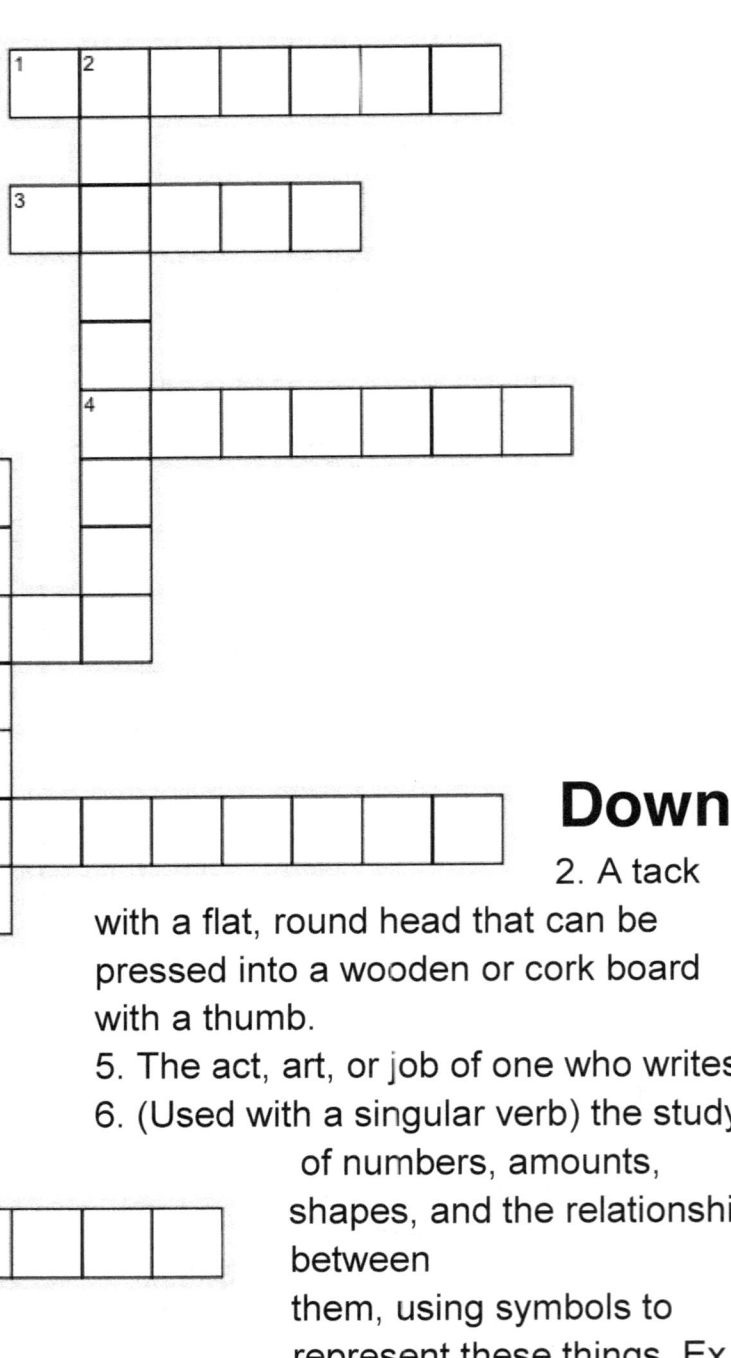

Down

2. A tack with a flat, round head that can be pressed into a wooden or cork board with a thumb.
5. The act, art, or job of one who writes.
6. (Used with a singular verb) the study of numbers, amounts, shapes, and the relationship between them, using symbols to represent these things. Ex. Arithmetic, algebra, and geometry.
8. The words of a language.

HALLOWEEN

Across

2. Unusual; odd; peculiar.
4. A creature in folk tales that is said to have died but come back to life. They suck blood from people in order to stay among the living.
7. A sudden and powerful scare; an upset of the mind or feelings.
8. A large, round, orange fruit that has a thick inside
pulp that can be eaten. They grow on vines.
9. A hole in which a dead body is buried; grave.

Down

1. A figure of a person made from stuffed clothes and placed in a field to scare birds away from crops.
3. A large, hairy spider found in the warmer parts of North, Central, and South America. Some of them have a slightly poisonous bite.
5. _____ or treat - A custom practiced at Halloween in which children visit their neighbors and say the words "_____ or treat" in order to receive a treat such as candy.
6. A ghost or something else that seems real, but is not real.
7. The dark image cast on some surface by a person or thing blocking the light of the sun or another source of light.

INSECT

Across

2. A very small insect without wings that lives on the bodies of people, birds, and other animals.
3. An insect whose lower body flashes with light at night. A kind of beetle.
7. An insect with a flat body and long antennae that lives in most parts of the world. Pests that live in homes and other buildings. All of them are active at night.
9. An insect with four large wings that flies mostly in the daytime. They are closely related to moths but have thinner bodies and are usually more brightly colored.
10. An insect that has broad wings and flies mostly at night. They look like butterflies, but they usually have thicker bodies and bushy antennae and are less colorful.

Down

1. An insect with a pair of hard front wings that covers a pair of thin wings. Ex. ladybugs, and fireflies.
4. A tiny insect that does not have wings but can jump far. They feed on the blood of the animals they bite.
5. A small, round beetle that is red or orange with black spots. They eat aphids and other insects that are harmful to plants.
6. A small animal related to the spider. It has a long narrow body and a tail with a poisonous tip. They live in many warm, dry areas of the world.
8. An insect that is related to a grasshopper. It has long antennae and strong hind legs for jumping. The male makes a chirping noise by rubbing his front wings together.

LOCATION

Across

3. A public road in a town or city along which vehicles travel. They are often have sidewalks and buildings along their sides.
8. A building with connected rooms in which people of the same family or group live.
9. A place where business or professional work is done.
10. A place where meals are prepared and served to customers.

Down

1. A place with many rooms and beds where people pay money to sleep, eat meals, or buy other services.
2. A country in western Europe. Paris is its capital city.
4. A place where sick or hurt people go to find care or help.
5. A place where goods are sold.
6. (Law) a room in which a lawcourt sits.
7. The earth's solid surface; land.

MATH

Across

1. To separate into parts.
4. One that expounds or interprets.
7. The word for the Roman numeral XV.
8. A number or amount added to another to form a sum.
9. A line that bends smoothly in one direction without any straight parts or angles.

Down

1. A group of twelve.
2. The word for the Roman numeral L.
3. The number in a fraction that is below the division line. It shows the number of equal parts into which the whole set is divided.
5. A line where two surfaces meet.
6. The line that forms the outside edge of a circle or other round figure or area.

SPORTS

Across

2. _____ line - a line or other marker indicating the end of a race.

6. The act of breaking a law or rule or doing something wrong; crime; sin.

8. A game played with a bat and ball by two teams of nine players each, the object being to score runs by advancing runners around four bases.

9. A baseball diamond, the positions at the four corners of the diamond, or the people playing those positions as a group.

10. One who fights, plays, or takes a position against another.

Down

1. A broadcast of a sports event or sports news on television or radio.

3. Relating to the game or match that comes just before the last one.

4. A tennis stroke that involves a forward movement of the arm with the back of the hand outward.

5. A member of the same team or group.

7. In football, either of two upright posts supported by a crossbar, defining an area through which a field goal or conversion must be kicked.

TOOLS

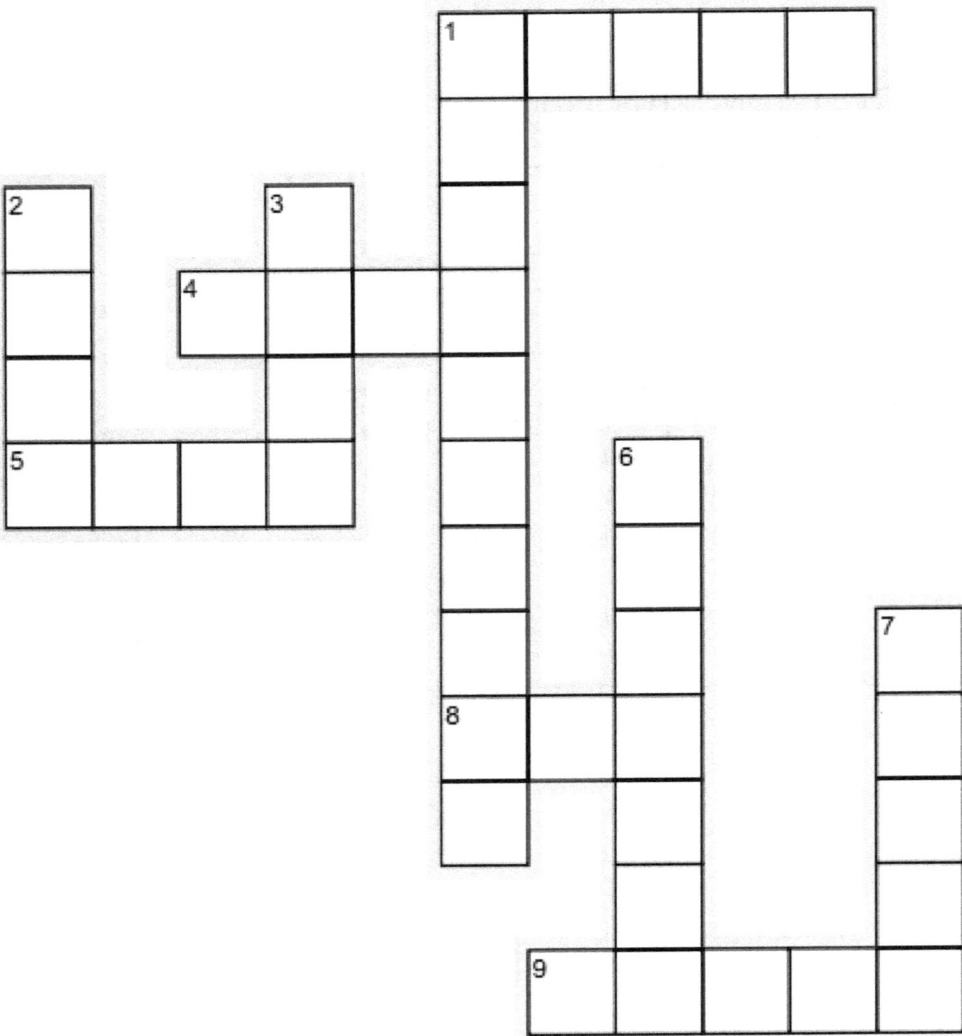

Across

1. ____ knife - A tool with a broad, flexible blade for applying putty.
4. ____ mower - A machine with a turning blade that cuts the grass of a lawn.
5. _____ measure - A tool for measuring length made of a long strip of cloth or flexible metal. It is marked off in inches, centimeters, or other units.
8. A tool with a thin metal blade that has sharp teeth along the edge. They are used for cutting hard materials such as wood or metal.
9. A tool with a shaft that has sharp cutting edges and is turned at a high speed to make holes in wood, metal, and other materials.

Down

1. A brush used to put paint on something.
2. A large wagon with two wheels pulled by animals and used to carry a heavy load.
3. A tool that has a long handle and a row of teeth or prongs at one end. It is used to gather hay or fallen leaves or to smooth down soil.
6. A heavy, metal bar or rod with a flattened and bent end. It is used to lift or pry things.
7. A tool used by carpenters to see if a surface is parallel to the ground.

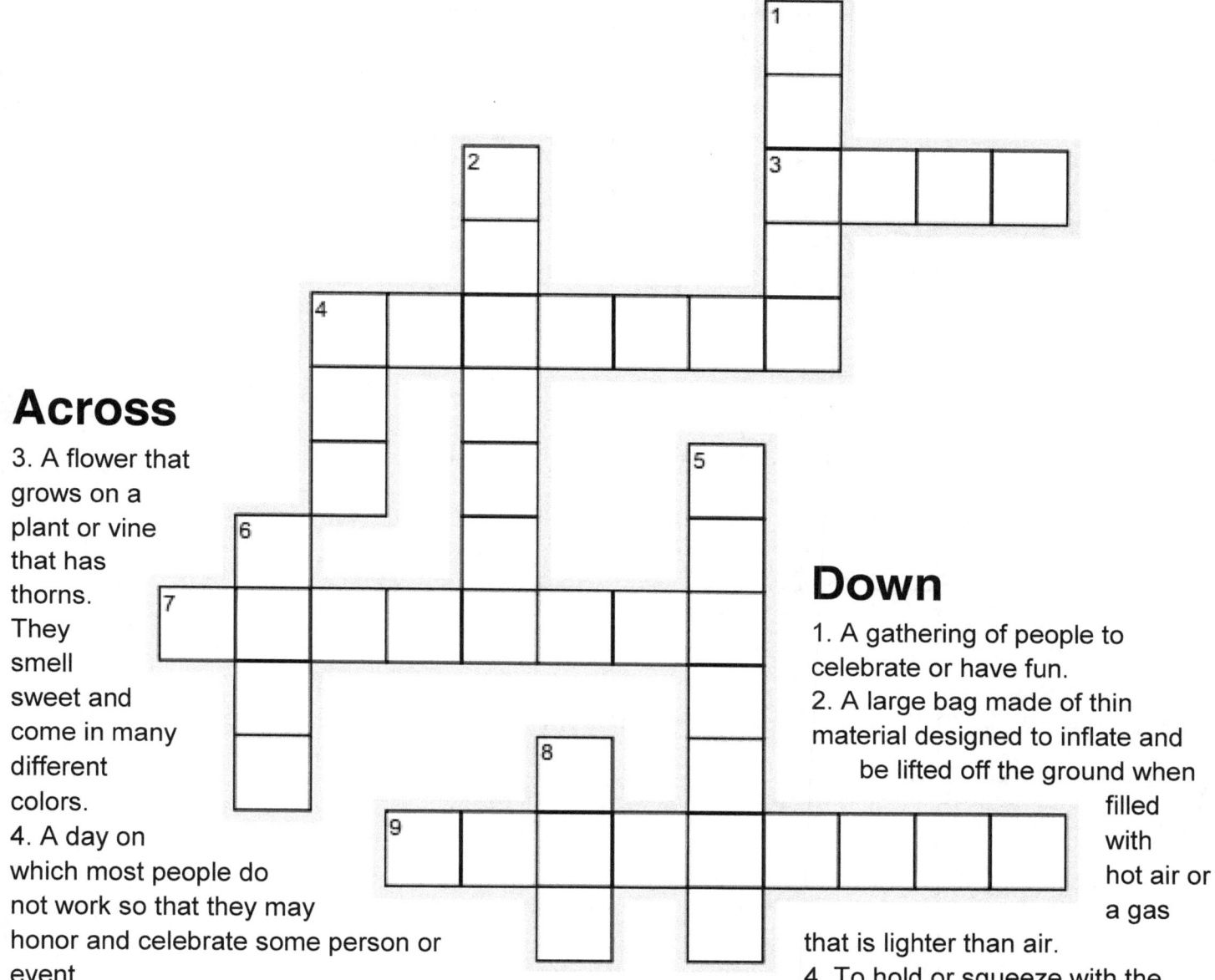

Across

3. A flower that grows on a plant or vine that has thorns. They smell sweet and come in many different colors.
4. A day on which most people do not work so that they may honor and celebrate some person or event.
7. The quality or condition of being fond.
9. A food substance that is made from ground cacao seeds. It is not sweet, but it is often used in candy and other sweet foods. It is also used in making certain kinds of sauces.

Down

1. A gathering of people to celebrate or have fun.
2. A large bag made of thin material designed to inflate and be lifted off the ground when filled with hot air or a gas that is lighter than air.
4. To hold or squeeze with the arms in a loving way; embrace.
5. Any strong feeling or emotion.
6. Strong feelings of affection for another person.
8. To seek to win the love or approval of, esp. as a spouse; court.

HALLOWEEN

Across

1. A frightening dream.
3. Inhabited or visited by ghosts.
7. The earth's natural satellite. It revolves around the earth from west to east in about 28 days.
8. To frighten.
9. Twelve o'clock at night.

Down

2. Frightening in a disgusting way; horrible.
4. Full of or relating to mystery.
5. A dress worn on special occasions.
6. A covering for the head worn for warmth, protection, or decoration.
10. To utter or make a long, loud, sad sound like that of a wolf or dog.

VIRTUES

Across

1. Adherence to standards of right conduct.
5. Kind understanding and concern for others when they are sad, suffering, or having trouble.
6. Not dirty or stained.
8. Giving help or aid.
9. A belief in the strength or truth of a person or thing.

Down

2. Having or showing respect; being polite.
3. A great feeling of happiness or pleasure; delight.
4. Arranged in a neat way; in order.
7. A class of people of noble rank.
8. A quality that makes people laugh or feel amused.

ADJECTIVES

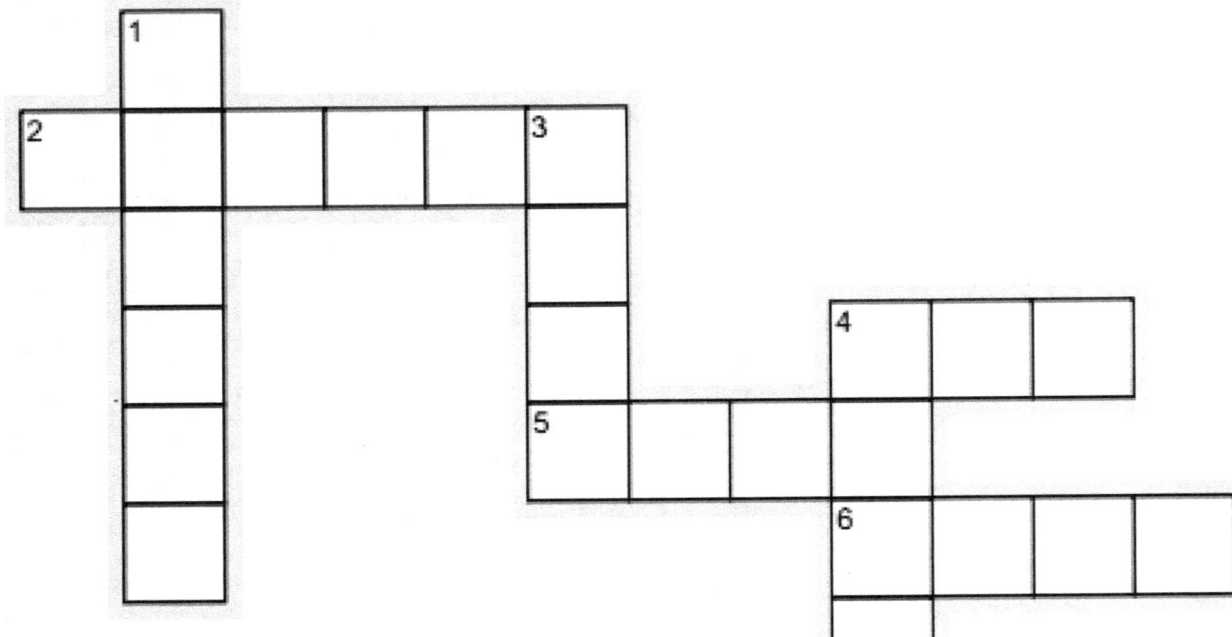

Across

2. Recognized or liked by the public.
4. Large in size, number, or weight.
5. Reaching across a large area from side to side.
6. Not having much physical strength or power.
7. (Comparative of 'good') superior to another (of the same class or set or kind) in excellence or quality or desirability or suitability; more highly skilled than another.
8. Not able to hear, or not able to hear well.

Down

1. Not wide or broad.
3. Not moving or not able to move quickly.
4. To enchant or cast a spell over with magic or as if with magic.
7. Not able to see; having no sight.

ANTONYMS

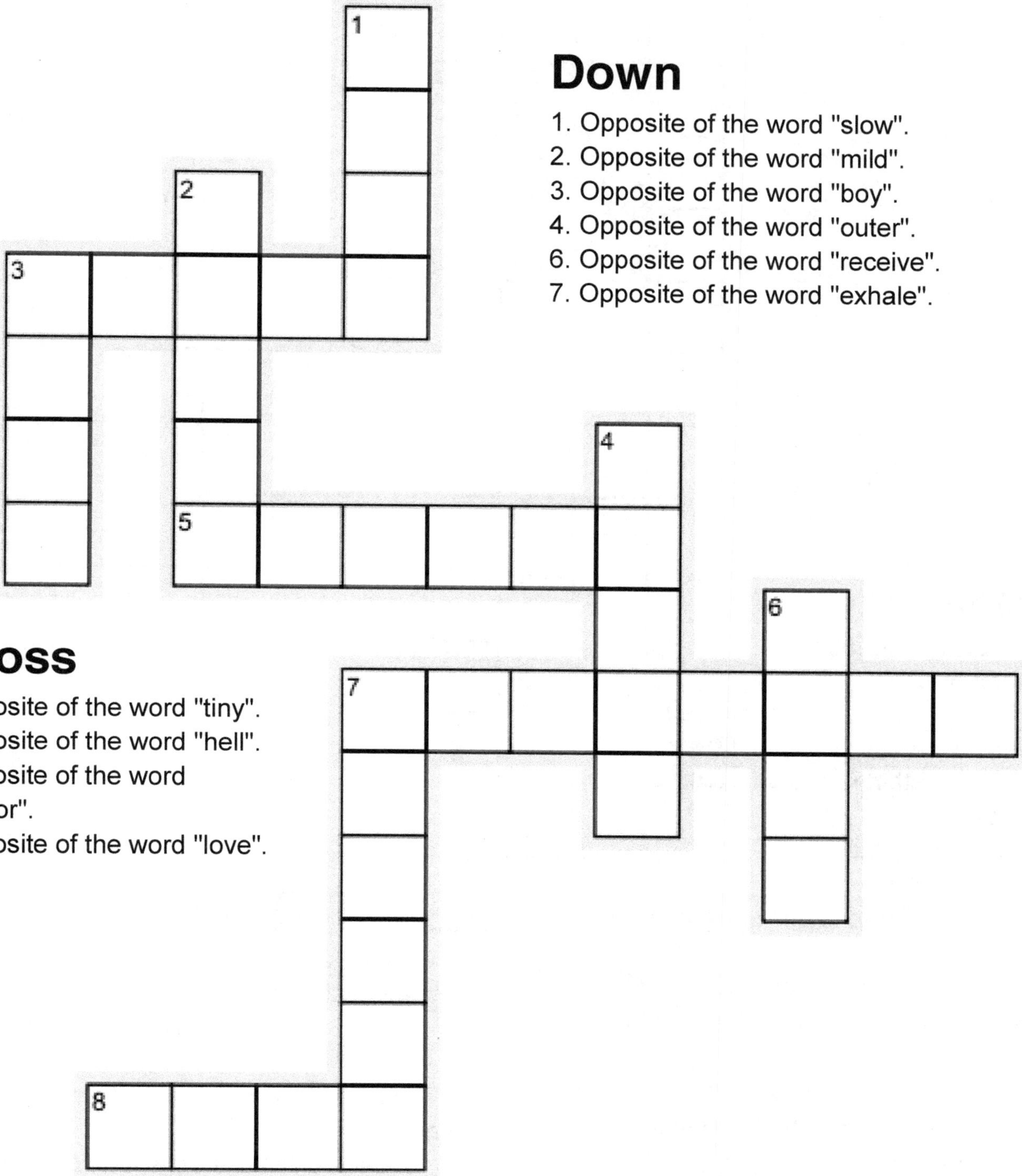

Down

1. Opposite of the word "slow".
2. Opposite of the word "mild".
3. Opposite of the word "boy".
4. Opposite of the word "outer".
6. Opposite of the word "receive".
7. Opposite of the word "exhale".

Across

3. Opposite of the word "tiny".
5. Opposite of the word "hell".
7. Opposite of the word "superior".
8. Opposite of the word "love".

BEACH

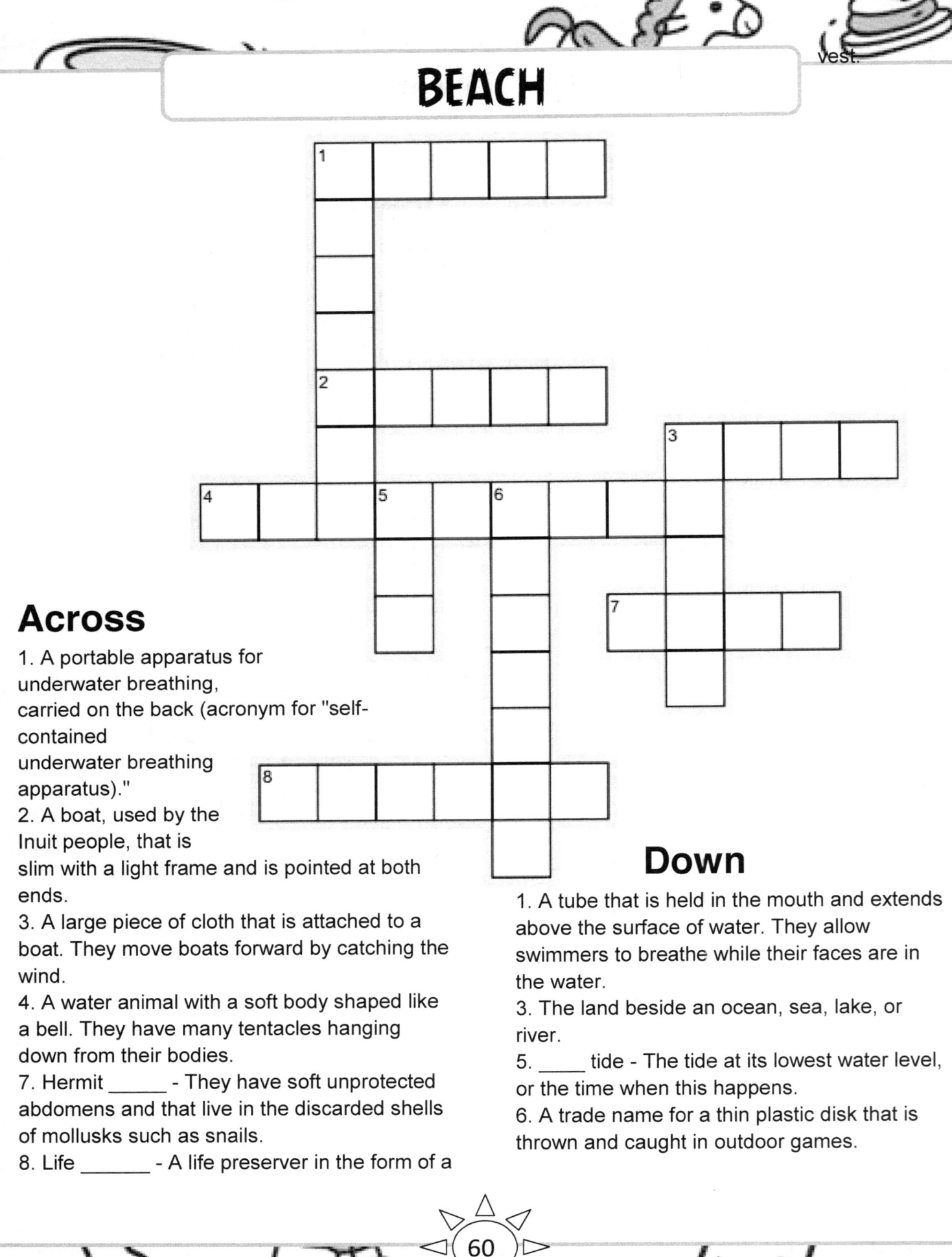

Across

1. A portable apparatus for underwater breathing, carried on the back (acronym for "self-contained underwater breathing apparatus)."

2. A boat, used by the Inuit people, that is slim with a light frame and is pointed at both ends.

3. A large piece of cloth that is attached to a boat. They move boats forward by catching the wind.

4. A water animal with a soft body shaped like a bell. They have many tentacles hanging down from their bodies.

7. Hermit _____ - They have soft unprotected abdomens and that live in the discarded shells of mollusks such as snails.

8. Life _____ - A life preserver in the form of a

Down

1. A tube that is held in the mouth and extends above the surface of water. They allow swimmers to breathe while their faces are in the water.

3. The land beside an ocean, sea, lake, or river.

5. _____ tide - The tide at its lowest water level, or the time when this happens.

6. A trade name for a thin plastic disk that is thrown and caught in outdoor games.

BIRTHDAY

Across

5. A valuable object that is greatly coveted and admired.
8. A building where food is prepared, sold and eaten.
10. To bring to the front of other objects, or to increase the importance of someone.

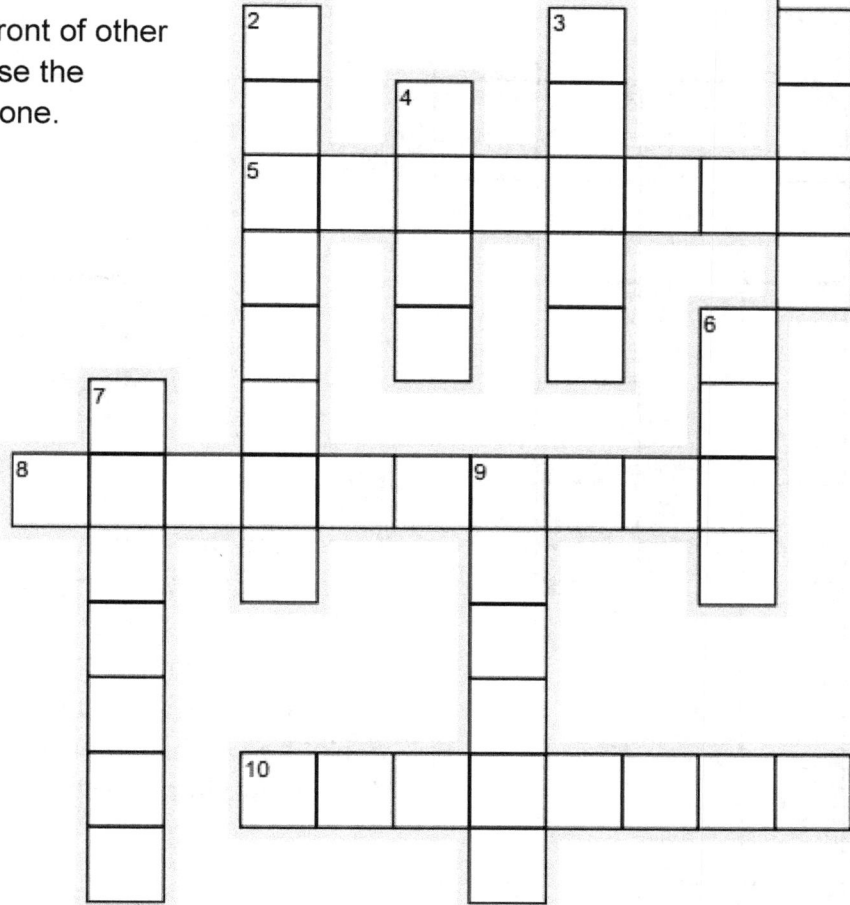

Down

1. When a present has been covered in paper.
2. Growing in knowledge and wisdom as someone gets older.
3. To go and see someone or something.
4. Has 365 days or 366 days.
6. Party _____ - Special brightly coloured head gear to wear at parties.
7. To be given something and to accept it.
9. Thin piece of brightly coloured fabric that is used to decorate a present.

ADJECTIVES

Across

2. Little in size, number, or amount.
4. Brave; daring.
6. Not joined or attached tightly; free.
8. Cracked or smashed into separate pieces, or no longer working.

Down

1. Of more than the average height.
2. Unhappy or without joy.
3. Of a size, or amount bigger than normal or average; not small.
4. Willing to give plenty; generous.
5. Not heavy, full, intense, or powerful.
7. Suffering from an illness; not well.

ANTONYMS

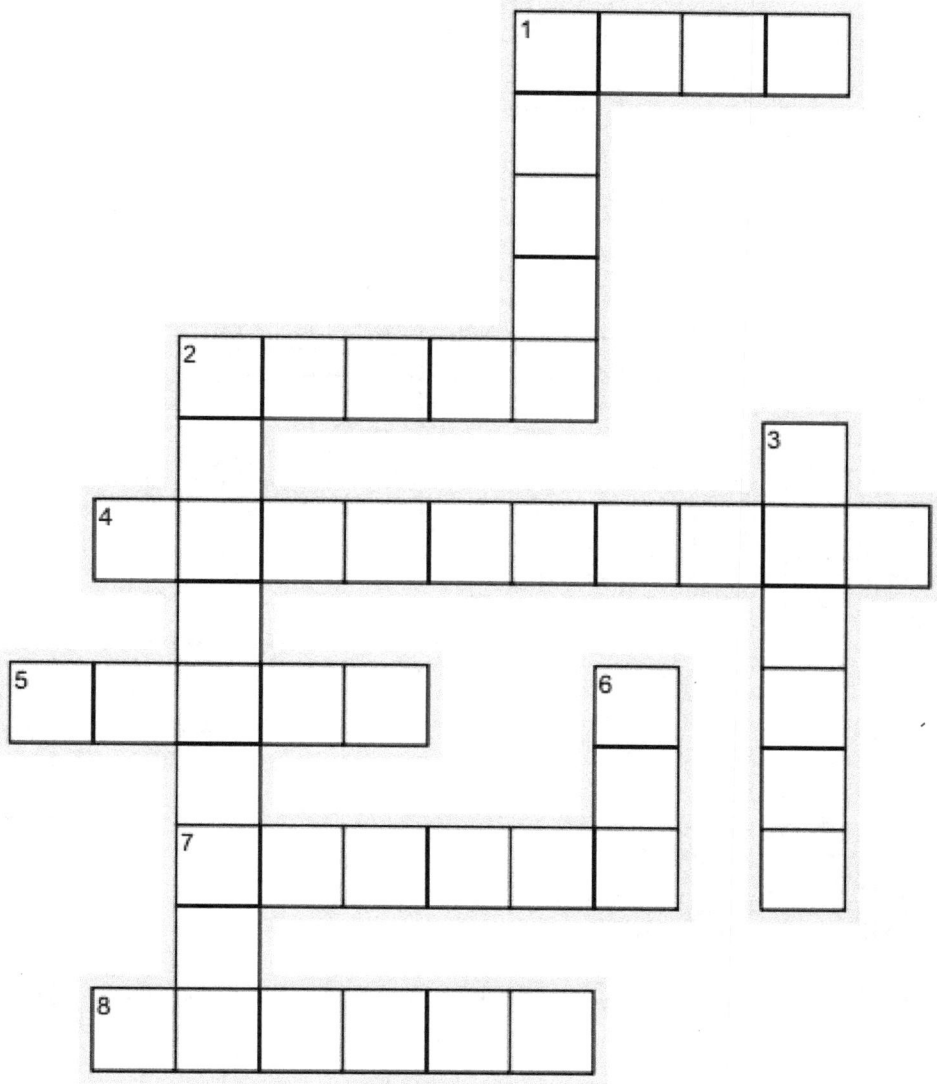

Across

1. Opposite of the word "aft".
2. Opposite of the word "sink".
4. Opposite of the word "natural".
5. Opposite of the word "lost".
7. Opposite of the word "disappear".
8. Opposite of the word "supply".

Down

1. Opposite of the word "last".
2. Opposite of the word "unfortunate".
3. Opposite of the word "unknown".
6. Opposite of the word "near".

BEACH

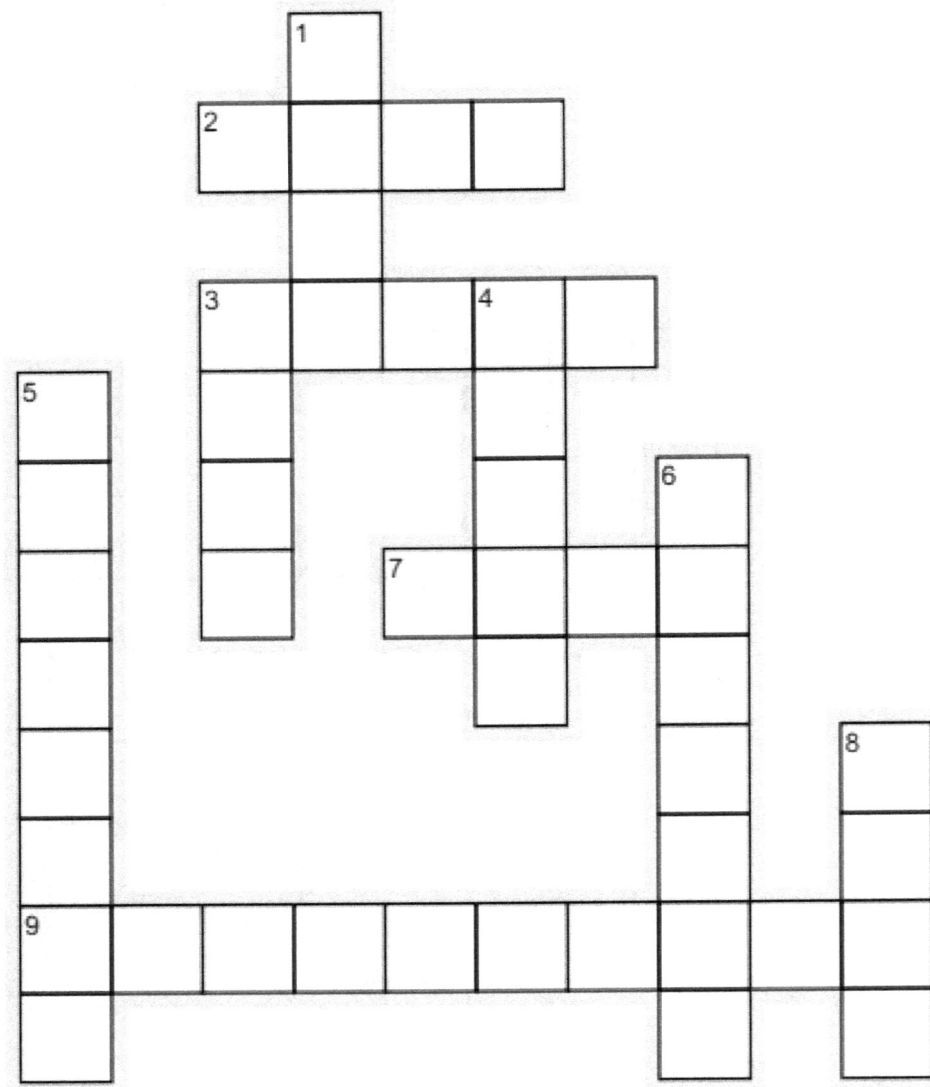

Down

1. _____ tide - The highest point reached by tide, or the time of day when this happens.
3. Tiny, loose grains of ground rock, found on beaches and in deserts.
4. To make looser or less stiff.
5. Any of various related tropical evergreens that grow in masses along tidal shores, with roots that grow above ground in a densely interlaced thicket.
6. A large water bird that lives in warm areas. It has a pouch in the lower half of its long bill for catching and holding fish.
8. _____ tree - Any of numerous, mainly tropical, evergreen plants, usu. unbranched and having a crown of large divided leaves, or fronds.

Across

2. To plunge or fall downward rapidly, usually head or front first.
3. A fish that lives in the ocean and has tough skin, large jaws and teeth, and a skeleton made of cartilage. Most of them eat other fish.
7. A large body of fresh or salt water that is surrounded on all sides by land.
9. A game in which two teams use their hands to hit a ball back and forth over a high net. Points are scored when the ball hits the ground in the opponent's court.

BUILDING

Across

3. A building where a large number of interesting and valuable objects, such as works of art or historical items, are kept, studied, and displayed to the public.
5. Even the good students say homework is what they most dislike about _____
7. A house made out of blocks of ice.
8. A small, simple shelter.
9. A place where goods are bought and sold, usually outdoors.

Down

1. Ancient stone buildings with four triangular sloping sides.
2. A large building with thick, high walls.
4. The door through which you can leave a public building.
5. A building or part of a building where things are sold.
6. Carries people and things up and down a tall building.

CLASSROOM

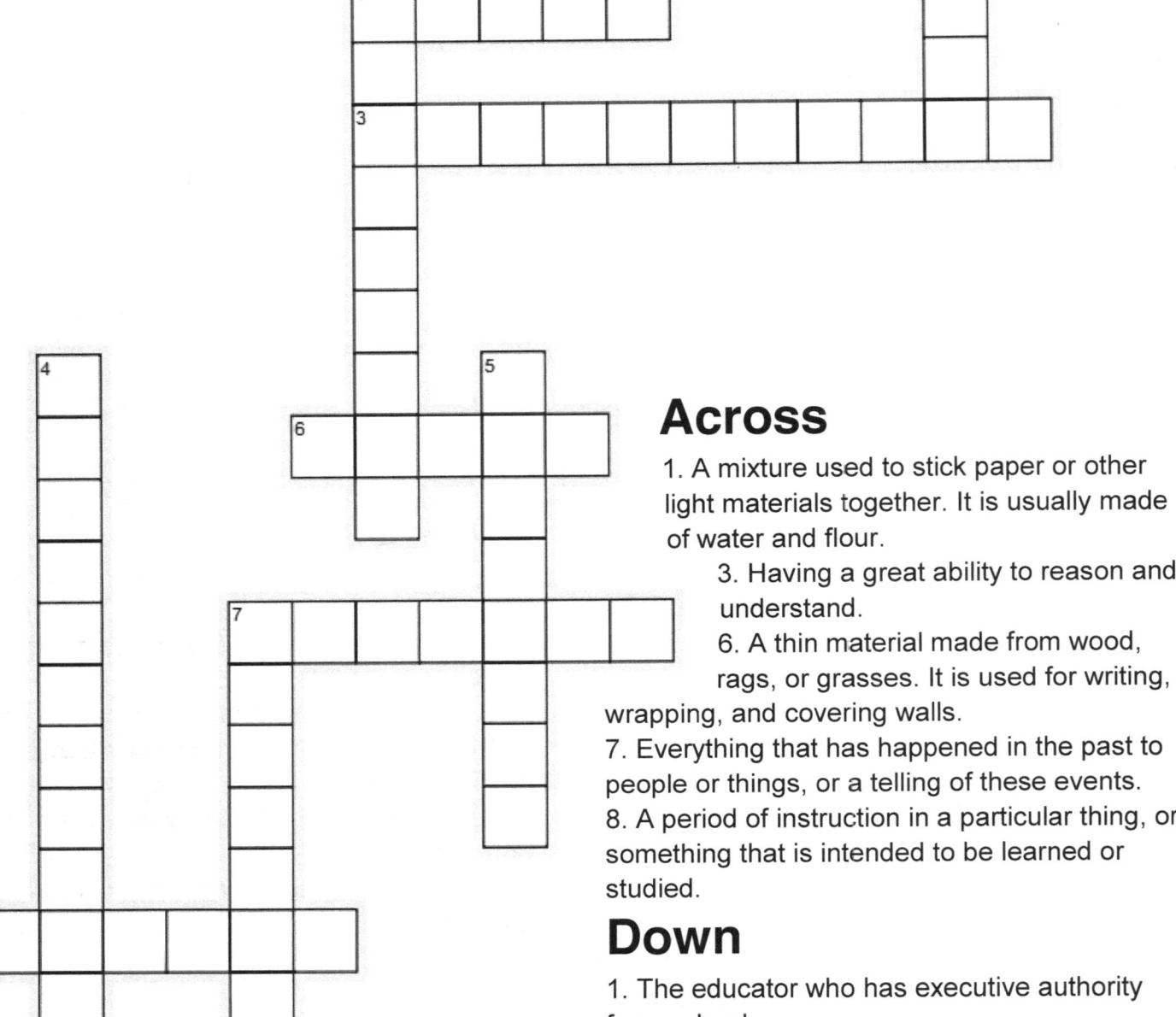

Across

1. A mixture used to stick paper or other light materials together. It is usually made of water and flour.

3. Having a great ability to reason and understand.

6. A thin material made from wood, rags, or grasses. It is used for writing, wrapping, and covering walls.

7. Everything that has happened in the past to people or things, or a telling of these events.

8. A period of instruction in a particular thing, or something that is intended to be learned or studied.

Down

1. The educator who has executive authority for a school.

2. A long, thin tool used for writing or drawing in ink.

4. A marker having a broad felt tip and transparent, often fluorescent ink, applied to lines of text to indicate their importance.

5. A row or rows of keys. Pianos, typewriters, and computers have it.

7. Schoolwork that is to be done at home rather than at school.

ADJECTIVES

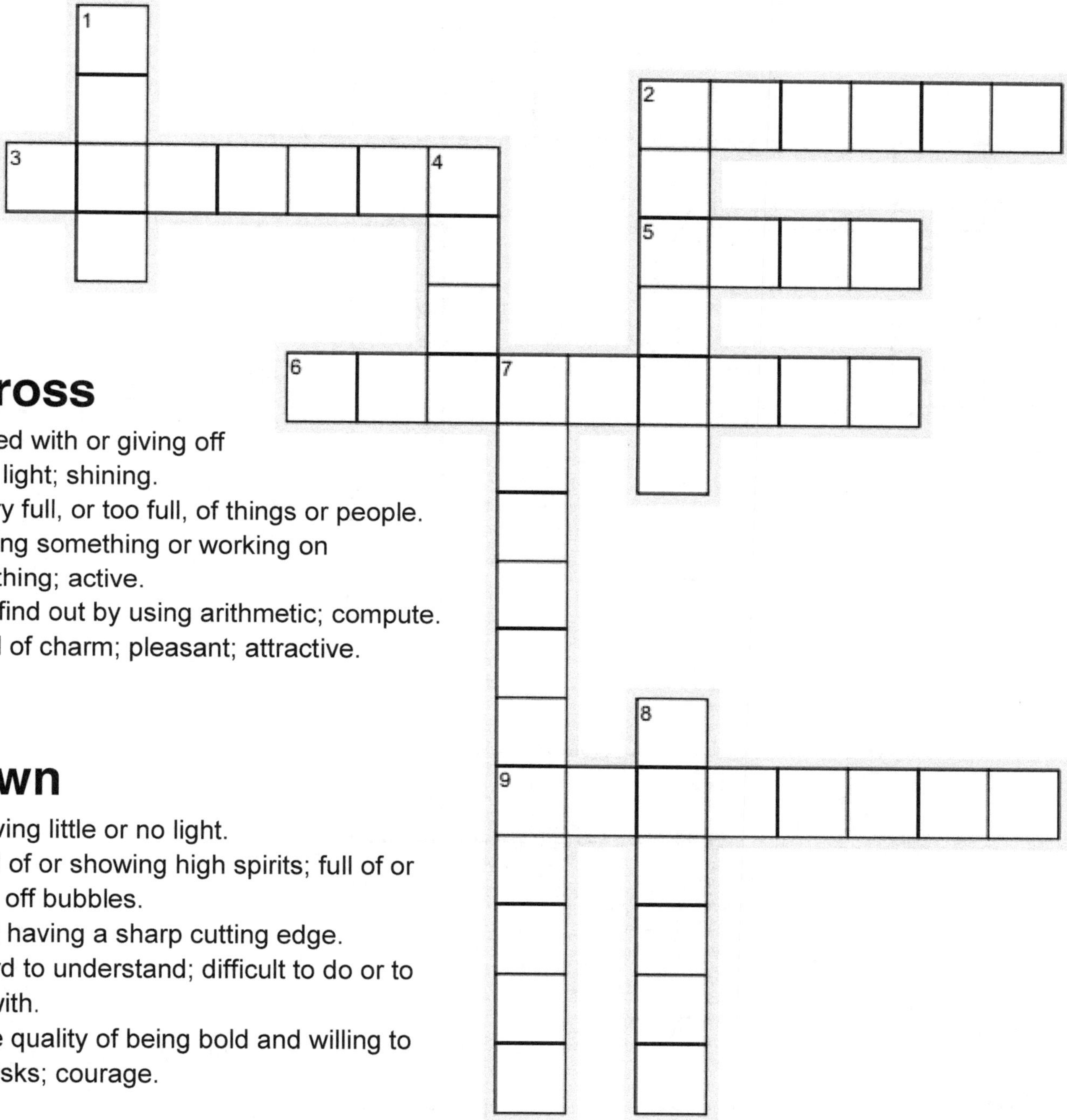

Across

2. Filled with or giving off much light; shining.
3. Very full, or too full, of things or people.
5. Doing something or working on something; active.
6. To find out by using arithmetic; compute.
9. Full of charm; pleasant; attractive.

Down

1. Having little or no light.
2. Full of or showing high spirits; full of or giving off bubbles.
4. Not having a sharp cutting edge.
7. Hard to understand; difficult to do or to deal with.
8. The quality of being bold and willing to take risks; courage.

ANTONYMS

Across

1. Opposite of the word "over".
3. Opposite of the word "go".
4. Opposite of the word "lose".
5. Opposite of the word " fake".
7. Opposite of the word "poor".

Down

1. Opposite of the word "down".
2. Opposite of the word " lower".
3. Opposite of the word "reap".
5. Opposite of the word "smooth".
6. Opposite of the word "weak".

BODY

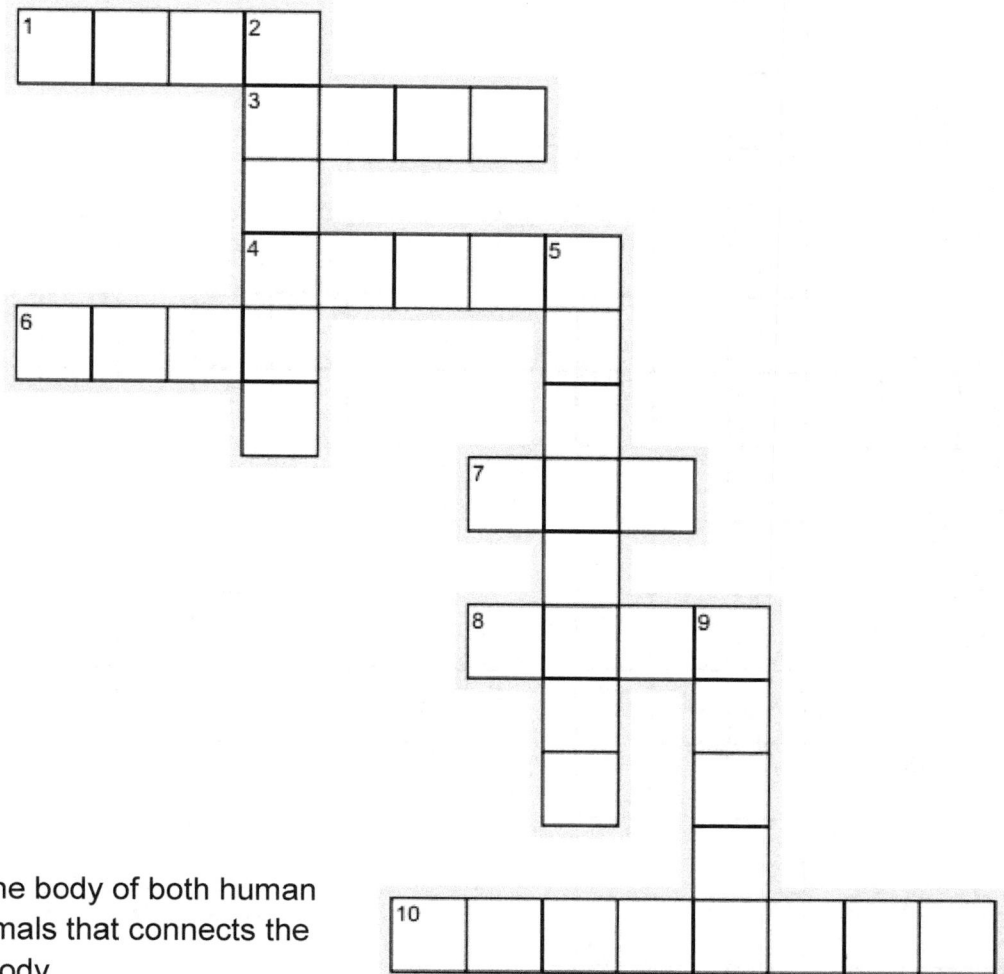

Across

1. The part of the body of both human beings and animals that connects the head with the body.
3. The colored circle around the pupil of the eye.
4. A round scar or hollow just below a person's waist. It is the spot where the umbilical cord was attached before the person's birth.
6. The joint between the upper and lower parts of a human leg.
7. Either or both of the two bones that frame the mouth and hold the teeth.
8. The rounded, back part of the human foot, or a part like it in an animal.
10. The part of the human face above the eyes and below the hair; brow.

Down

2. One of a pair of organs in the body which remove water and waste products from the blood. The waste products go from the _____ to the bladder in the form of urine.
5. A band of tough tissue that connects bones or supports muscles or organs.
9. A slightly yellowish liquid produced by body tissues. It contains many white blood cells.

CLASSROOM

Across

3. A person who is taught by a teacher.
4. To form on a surface with a pen, pencil, typewriter, or other instrument.
6. A sentence that asks for a reply.
7. A tool used for cutting. They are made up of two blades that are joined so that their edges may be opened and closed.
8. A board, usually colored white, used as a writing surface in places such as classrooms and meeting rooms.

Down

1. To make or become sharp.
2. A semicircular instrument with graduated markings, used in mathematics, surveying, and the like to construct and measure angles.
3. A portable case for transporting unbound papers or other printed material.
5. A relaxing break from an activity, such as school classes or trials in court.
7. Clever; intelligent.

ADJECTIVES

Across

2. Causing or able to cause death.
3. To not do or not succeed in doing; be unable.
4. Having power, force, or effectiveness.
5. Turned into ice; affected by freezing or by long and severe cold.
8. Full of energy; active.
9. Having knowledge and spiritual insight

Down

1. Able to return to its original form after being stretched or squeezed.
3. Covered with or having flowers; flowered.
6. Fine or rich in quality.
7. Honest, direct, and open.

ANTONYMS

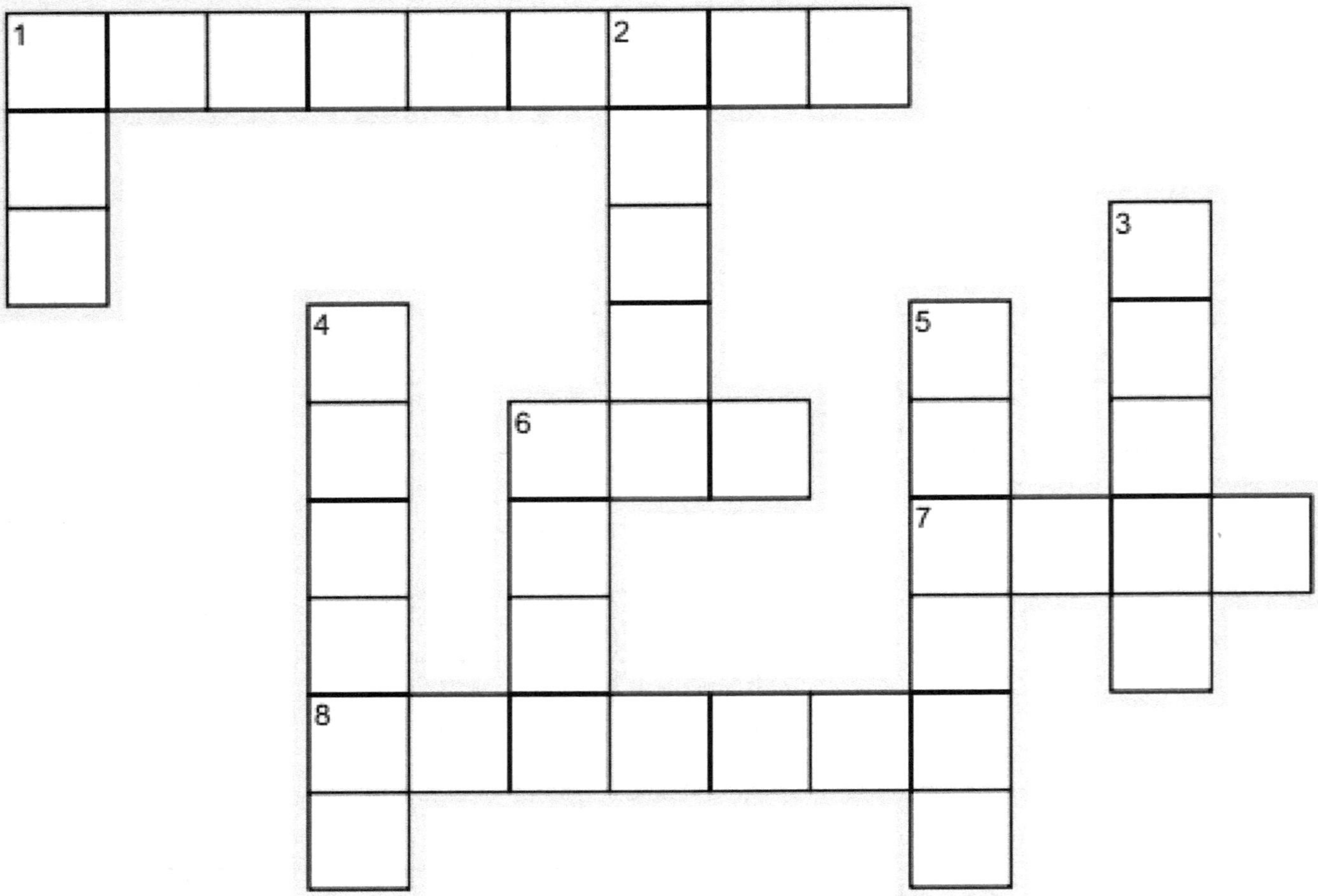

Across

1. Opposite of the word "appear".
6. Opposite of the word "wet".
7. Opposite of the word "hot".
8. Opposite of the word "known".

Down

1. Opposite of the word "night".
2. Opposite of the word "exit".
3. Opposite of the word "late".
4. Opposite of the word "useless".
5. Opposite of the word "occupied".
6. Opposite of the word "light".

BODY

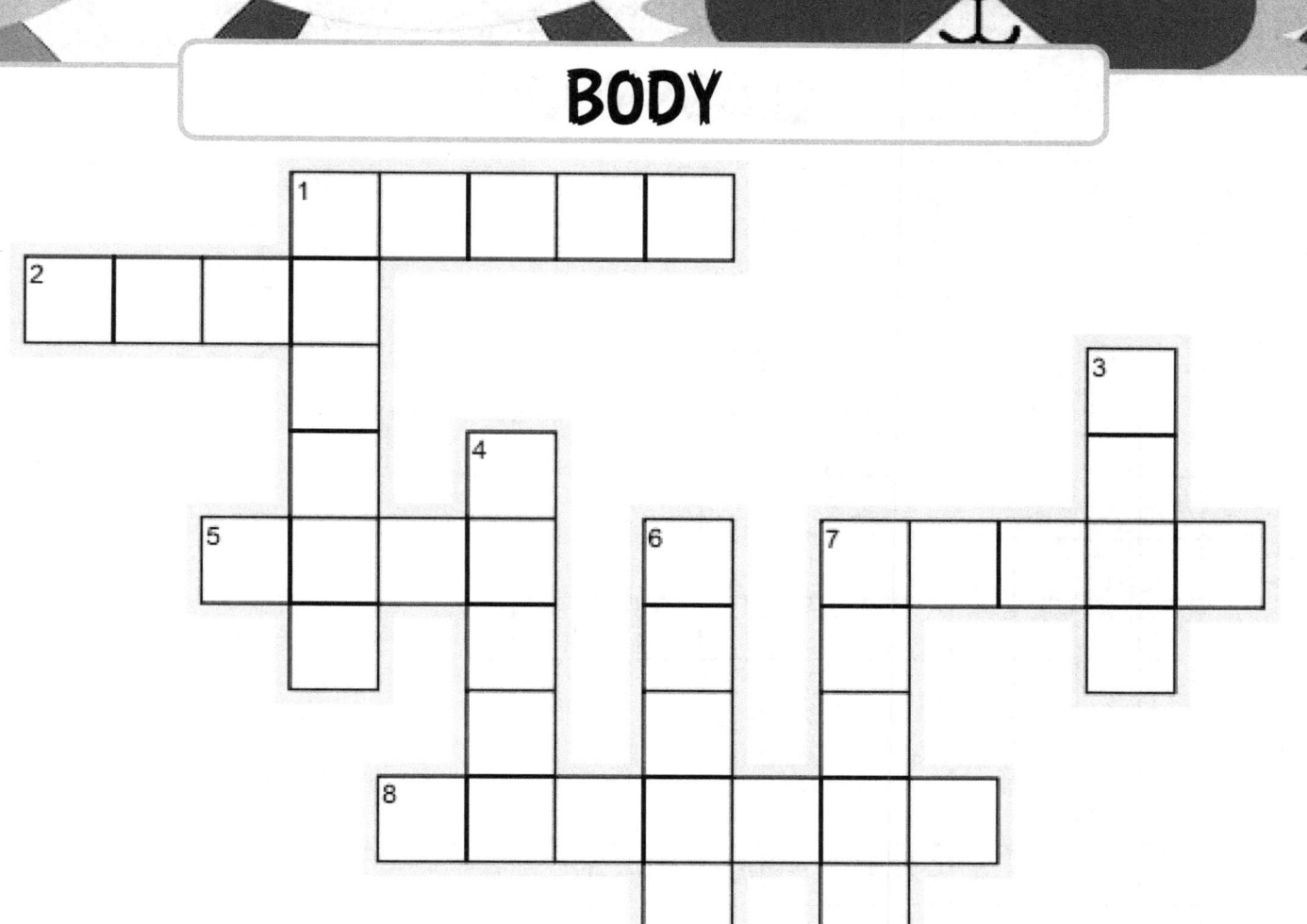

Across

1. The short, thick first finger on humans and other primates. It makes it easy for the hand to pick up things and grasp them.
2. The bottom of something that comes in contact with the ground. Feet and shoes have them.
5. A tiny opening in the skin of an animal or outer surface of a plant through which air, water, or sweat may pass.
7. The bony framework of the head and face that protects the brain.
8. The cavity and surrounding muscles and tissue located between the back of the nose and throat and the esophagus.

Down

1. A cord or band of tough white tissue that connects a muscle with a bone or other body part; sinew.
3. The inner surface of the hand, between the wrist and the base of the fingers.
4. Plural of tooth.
6. The organ in a female animal that produces eggs and certain hormones.
7. The backbone; spinal column.

CLASSROOM

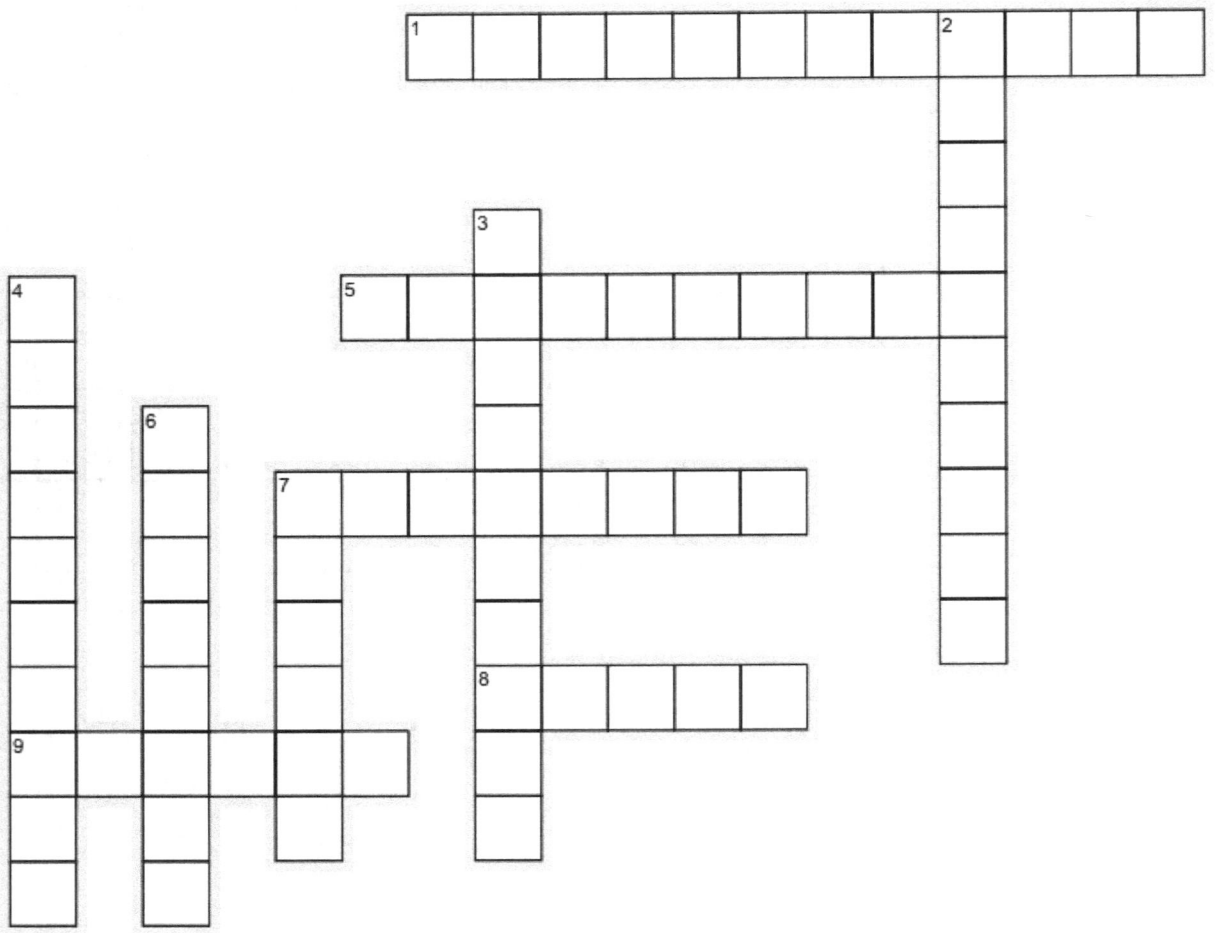

Across

1. A book or set of books that has information on a wide variety of subjects, or on many aspects of one subject.
5. A machine or computer application used in calculating or computing numbers.
7. A pack used to carry objects on one's back while hiking or walking.
8. A book of maps, tables, or charts.
9. An object used to erase or rub out writing or marks.

Down

2. A carefully planned test used to discover something unknown.
3. A smooth, hard panel for writing on with chalk; chalkboard.
4. An assigned task, such as a job or lesson.
6. A strip of leather, ribbon, or paper placed between pages to mark a place in a book.
7. A large, sturdy notebook cover that contains a device for holding loose papers.

HALLOWEEN

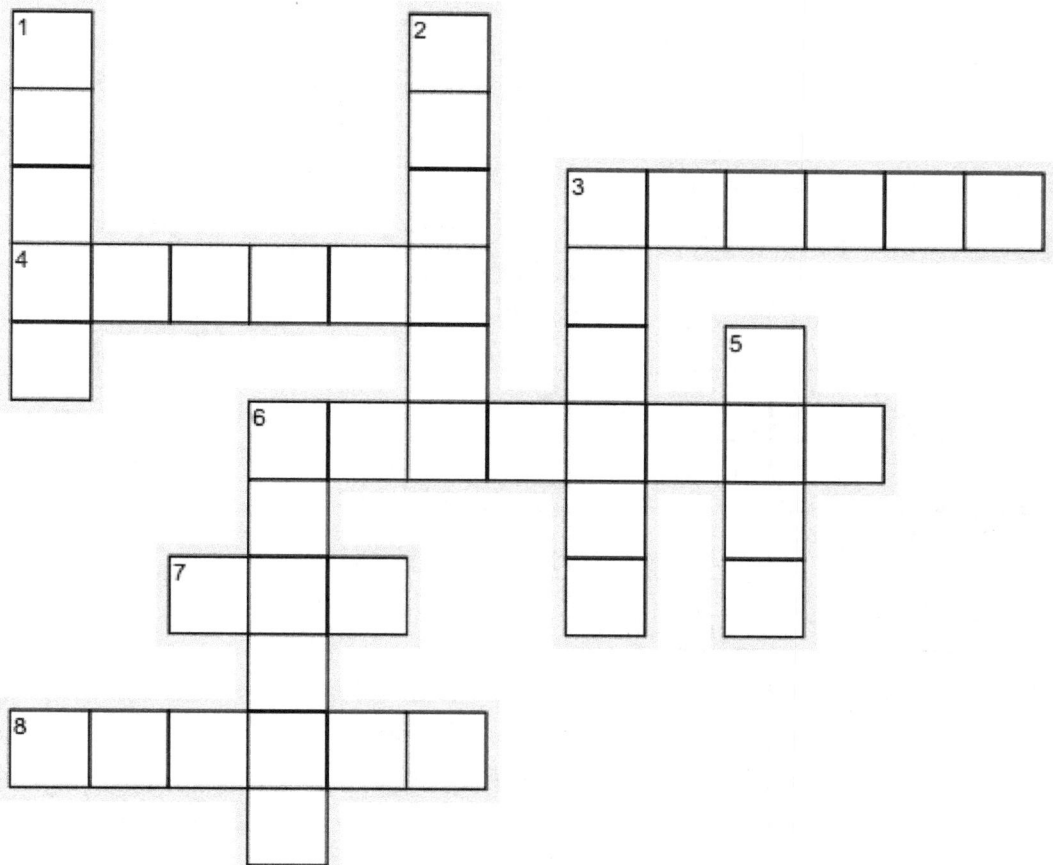

Across

3. A box in which a dead person is buried.
4. A web spun by a spider, or a single piece of this web.
6. The inner framework of bones and cartilage in vertebrate animals. They support the body and protect softer body parts.
7. A head covering made of natural or artificial hair, worn to cover one's own hair.
8. Lipstick, powder, and other cosmetics put on the face to change the way it looks or to make it look better.

Down

1. A woman who is believed to have magic powers.
2. A spell or supernatural force that, according to voodoo belief and legend, can enter a corpse, return life to it, and then control its actions.
3. Of or causing a feeling of anxiety, fear, or disgust similar to that which might be produced by something crawling on one's skin.
5. Without heat or warmth.
6. A small animal with eight legs and a body made up of two parts. Most of them spin webs in which they nest and catch insects to eat.

ADJECTIVES

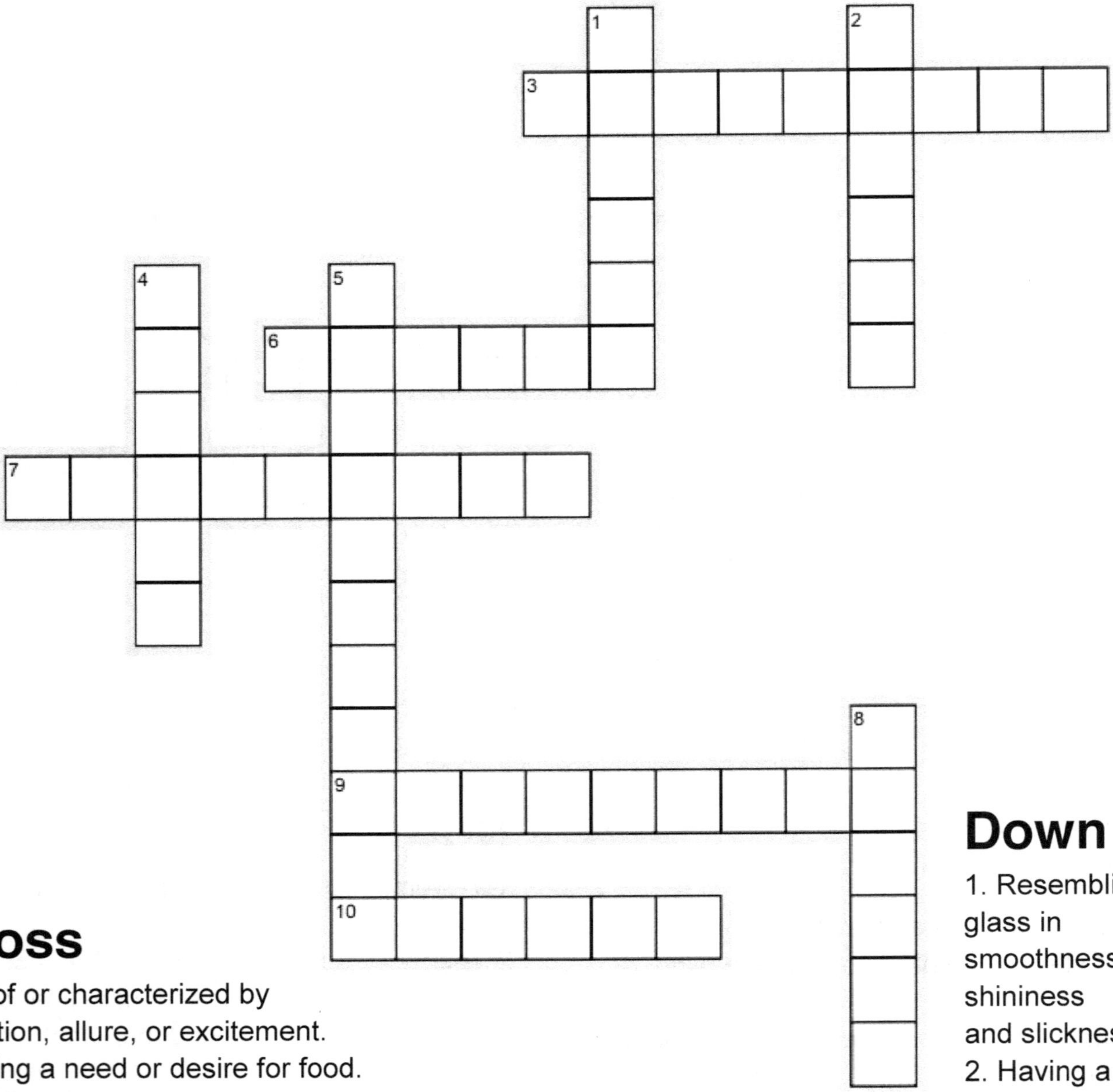

Across

3. Full of or characterized by fascination, allure, or excitement.
6. Feeling a need or desire for food.
7. Very funny.
9. Exactly alike; incapable of being perceived as different; the same.
10. Having a special talent or ability.

Down

1. Resembling glass in smoothness and shininess and slickness
2. Having a very strong desire for ever more money or things.
4. Having an empty space on the inside; not solid within.
5. Causing feelings of shame, disgrace, or deep embarrassment.
8. Having a smooth, shiny surface or appearance.

ANTONYMS

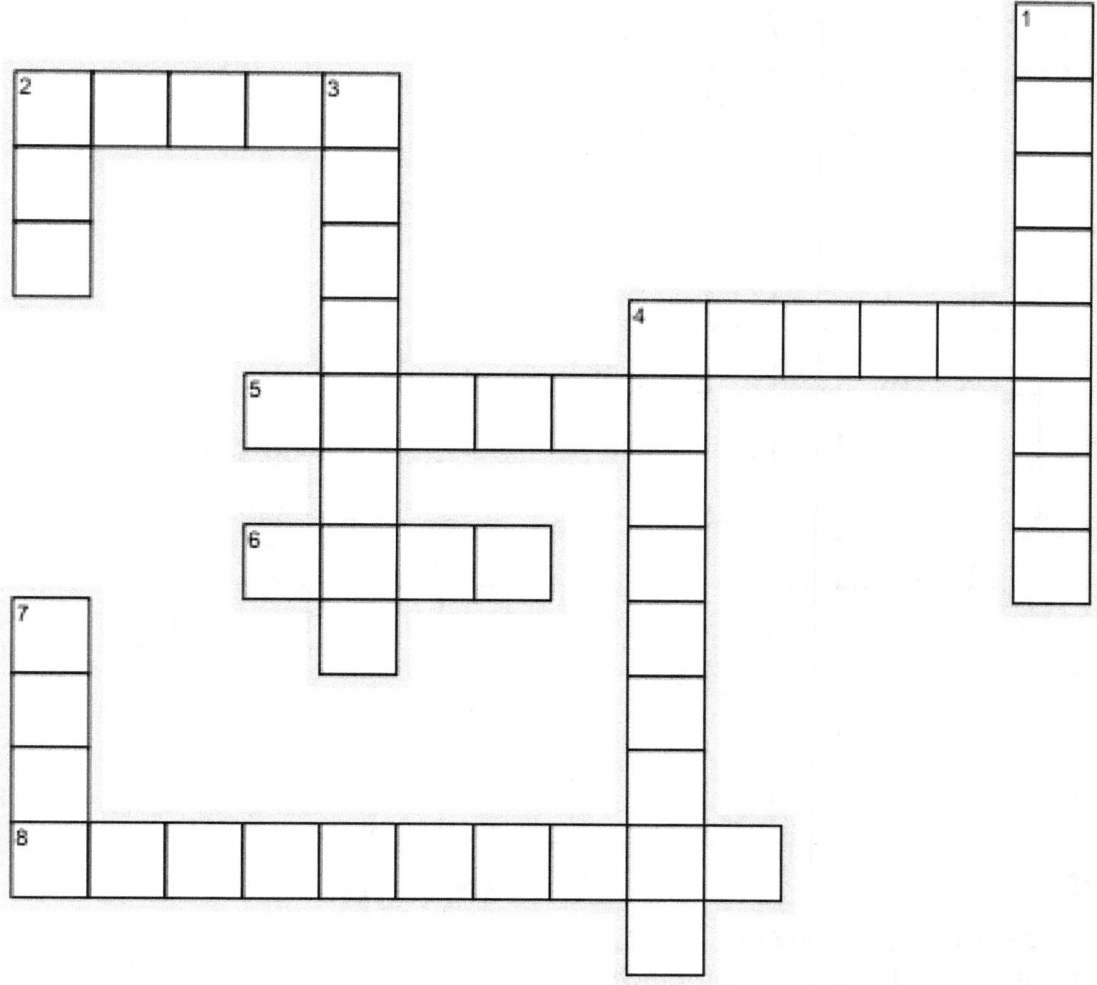

Across

2. Opposite of the word "true".
4. Opposite of the word "question".
5. Opposite of the word "enemy".
6. Opposite of the word "succeed".
8. Opposite of the word "encourage".

Down

1. Opposite of the word "inaccurate".
2. Opposite of the word "thin".
3. Opposite of the word "internal".
4. Opposite of the word "disadvantage".
7. Opposite of the word "unfold".

BODY

Across

2. The narrow passage inside the neck. Food and air pass through the throat to the stomach and lungs.
4. The part of the human leg between the hip and the knee.
5. The small, dark opening in the center of the eye. Light passes through it to the eye.
7. The human body from neck to hips; trunk.
8. The inner framework of bones and cartilage in vertebrate animals. They support the body and protect softer body parts.
9. A large gland near the stomach. It makes digestive juices and insulin.

Down

1. The nail on a toe, esp. a human toe.
3. The part of the human body between the chest and hips.
4. One tear.
6. The muscular organ of a female mammal in which the fetus develops before birth.

CLASSROOM

Across

3. A test of skill used to see how much a person knows or can do.

5. A room in a school or college where classes are held.

7. A piece of paper or cardboard folded at the center. It can hold papers or letters.

8. The science of the earth's surface and all life on it. You'll learn about the different countries and people of the earth, its climate, its natural resources, and its oceans, rivers, and mountains.

10. A piece of furniture with drawers and a flat surface used for reading and writing.

Down

1. A list of unusual or difficult words and their meanings connected with a particular subject or particular piece of writing. It is often placed at the end of a book.

2. Sheets of paper bound together between two covers. These pages can be blank or can have writing, printing, or pictures on them.

4. To learn completely so as to hold in the memory.

6. A place where books, records, and other materials are kept and from which they may be borrowed.

9. A level, degree, or rank in a scale.

HALLOWEEN

Across

3. To change or hide the looks of in order to prevent recognition.
6. A female ballet dancer.
7. A long, loose, outer garment without sleeves.
8. Mysterious and frightening; weird.
9. An imaginary, frightening man that supposedly carries away disobedient children.

Down

1. The type of clothing worn in a particular place or time or by members of a particular group.
2. In a late nineteenth-century novel by Bram Stoker, the title character, a vampire, who is able to transform himself into a bat.
4. To cause fear in; scare.
5. The red liquid containing oxygen and nutrients that pumps through the veins and arteries of humans and many other animals.
7. A sweet food made of sugar and flavorings such as chocolate or peppermint.

SPORTS

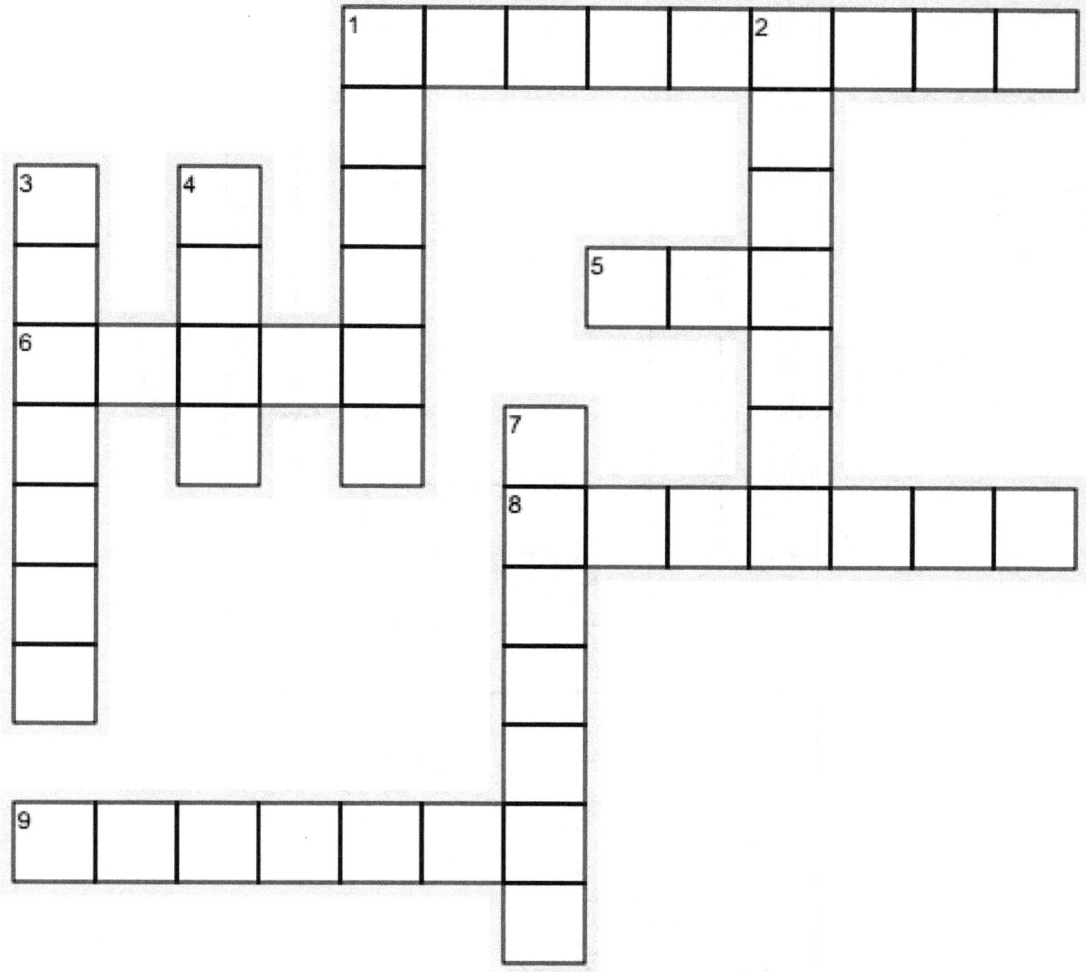

Across

1. The act of scoring six points in football by catching or carrying the ball behind the opponent's goal line.
5. Finish a game with an equal number of points, goals, etc.
6. (Sport) someone in charge of training an athlete or a team.
8. A sports official who makes sure that players follow the rules of the game.
9. Run with the ball, in basketball bouncing the ball or in soccer or hockey making small kicks.

Down

1. Something given to recognize a win or other accomplishment; award.
2. The act of protecting or guarding.
3. A kick in football that puts the ball into action and signals the beginning or continuing of the game.
4. A result or end that a person wants and works for; aim or purpose.
7. A person who trains people or horses so they are strong and ready for competition.

MATH

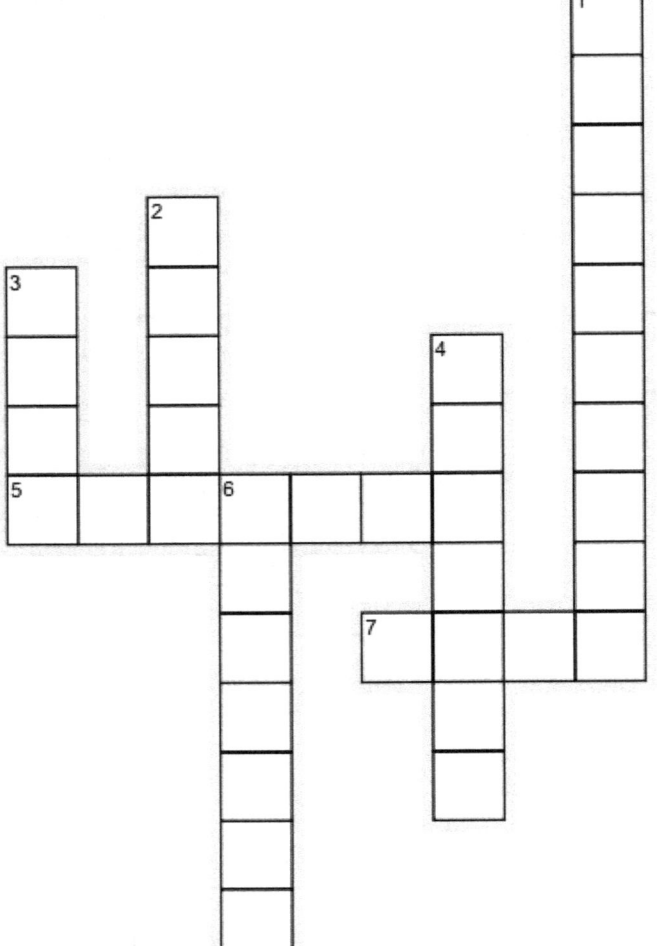

Across

5. A shape that looks like a flattened circle; oval.
7. A particular day or point in time.
8. A unit of length equal to one twelfth of a foot or 2.54 centimeters. (abbreviated: in.)
9. A real or imaginary line through the center of an object, around which the object turns.
10. To list or name one by one in order to find the total.

Down

1. A pair of numbers that identifies a point on a graph or grid; ordered pair.
2. Having the same value, measure, or amount as something else.
3. The product of a number multiplied by itself twice.
4. The number gotten by adding two or more quantities and then dividing that result by the number of quantities added.
6. The point or place where two or more lines, roads, or other straight things meet.

ADJECTIVES

Across

3. Of or having to do with what happens between two or more countries; Concerning or belonging to all or at least two or more nations
5. Liked by others, or easy to like.
9. Having a lasting effect on the mind or feelings; making a strong impression.
10. Having information or knowledge; familiar.

Down

1. Free from evil or knowledge of evil.
2. Causing an irritating cutaneous sensation; being affect with an itch.
4. Continuing for a long time, not ending.
6. Not polite; rude.
7. Full of joy; happy.
8. Highest in rank or most important; principal; main.

ANTONYMS

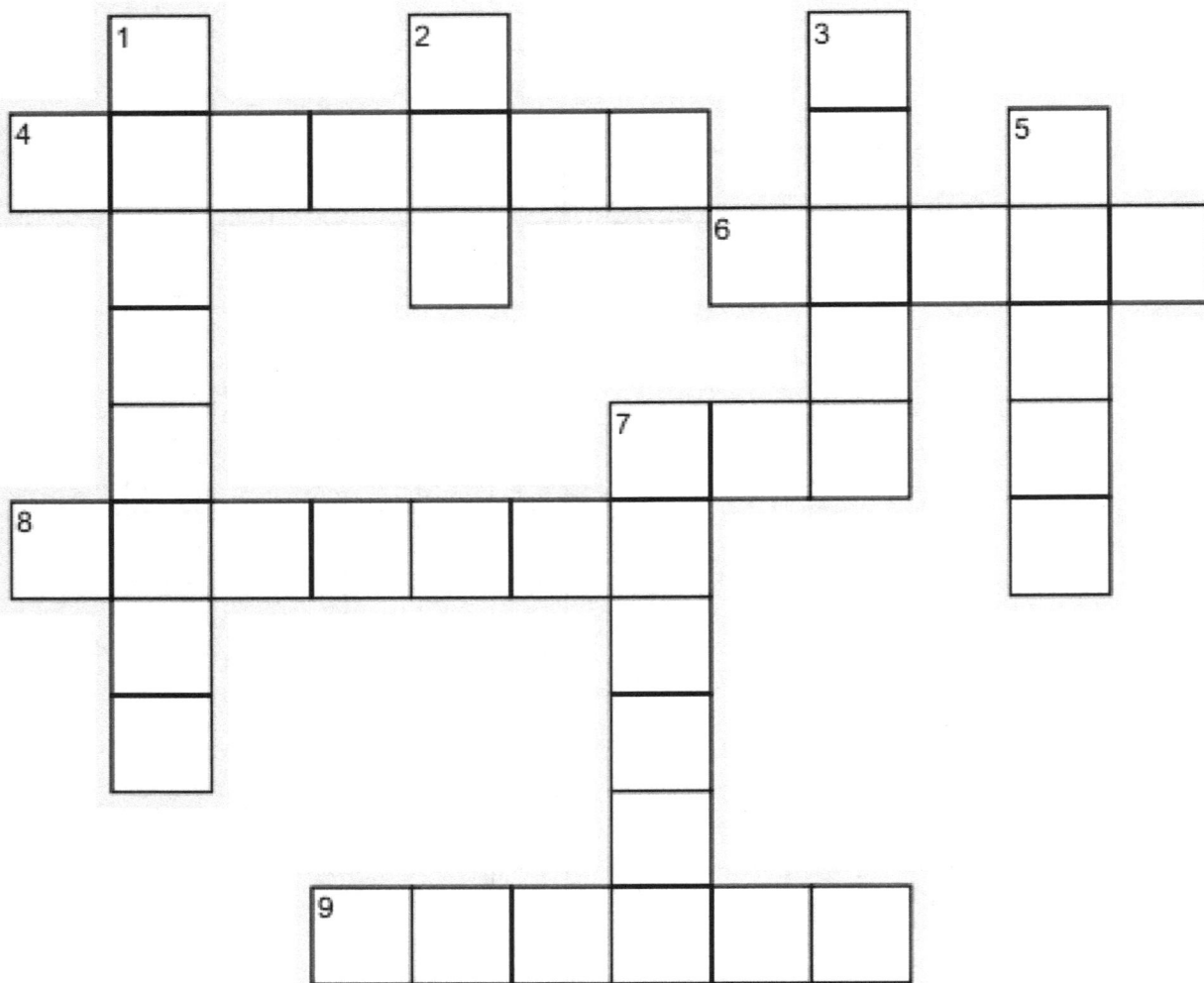

Across
4. Opposite of the word "free".
6. Opposite of the word "destroy".
7. Opposite of the word "little".
8. Opposite of the word "incapable".
9. Opposite of the word "lend".

Down
1. Opposite of the word "forward".
2. Opposite of the word "yang".
3. Opposite of the word "old".
5. Opposite of the word "white".
7. Opposite of the word "worse".

BODY

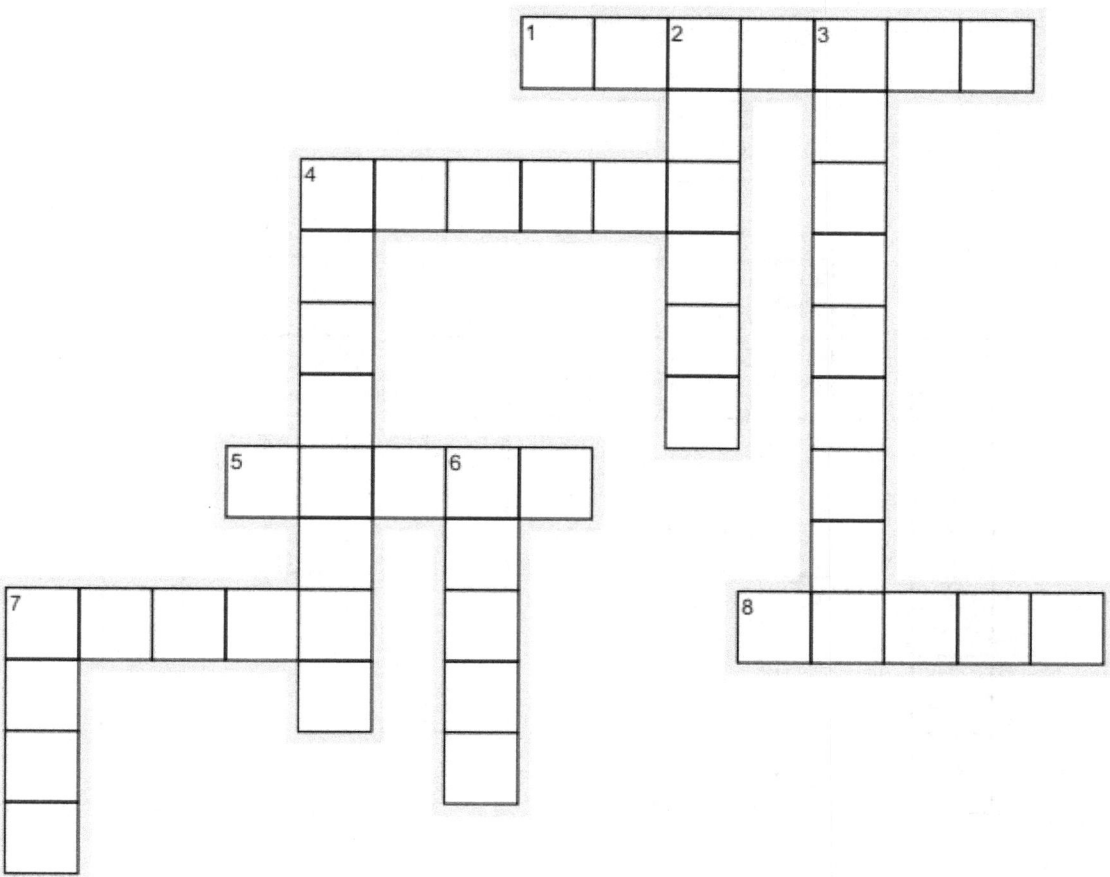

Across

1. An organ inside the body that collects urine. It gets larger when it fills and smaller when it becomes empty.
4. The front part of the body between the neck and the stomach; chest.
5. _____ cord - Either of two pairs of folds of mucous membrane projecting into the larynx
7. Either side of the face between the nose and the ear.
8. The front of a person or underside of an animal; stomach.

Down

2. A blood vessel that carries blood away from the heart.
3. Of or relating to digestion.
4. The rounded parts of the human body at the base of the spine that are used to sit on.
6. Adam's _____ - The lump in the throat, usually more noticeable in men than in women.
7. The rounded back part of a human's leg below the knee.

CLASSROOM

Across

2. A long narrow strip of plastic, cloth, or paper that has glue on one side. It is used to stick things together.
4. A set of questions to find out how much someone knows about something, or their ability to do something.
6. A person who goes to a school or college.
9. A system of studying, testing, and experimenting on things in nature. It is a search for general laws about how the world works.

Down

1. A piece of furniture with a flat top supported by one or more legs.
3. The action or activity of examining and understanding written language.
5. To question in order to test knowledge.
6. A place for teaching and learning.
7. To use the power of the mind.
8. A book that lists words with their synonyms or antonyms.

HALLOWEEN

Across

2. A person who is believed to have magic powers.
5. A mixture for drinking that is supposed to have special powers. It may heal, do magic, or be a poison.
7. A small, ugly creature in fairy tales that does evil or mischief to humans.
8. In folklore, a person who has changed into or is capable of changing into a wolf and back into a human again; lycanthrope.
9. A word or group of words used to work magic.

Down

1. To live in or visit as a ghost.
3. A large, frightening imaginary creature.
4. A teasing trick; stunt.
6. The light of the moon.
8. Evil in actions or ideas.

BODY

Across

3. One of the two outside openings in the nose.
6. Having to do with or used in the act of breathing.
8. A knoblike or knotlike swelling or mass of tissue.
9. A rounded projection, such as that at the base of the ear.

Down

1. A small, two-lobed gland of vertebrates that is located at the base of the brain and produces important metabolic and developmental hormones.
2. A large tooth located in the back of the mouth, with a broad biting surface used for grinding food.
4. A large, reddish brown organ in the body that has many functions. It cleans the blood, stores energy and nutrients, makes bile, and helps the body digest fats. It is found at the top of the abdomen.
5. Either of the upper or lower edges of flesh that circle the mouth and are used in speech.
7. Protected from a disease, either naturally or by getting a vaccine.
9. The structure at the top of the windpipe that contains the vocal cords, which produce the human voice; voice box.

VERB

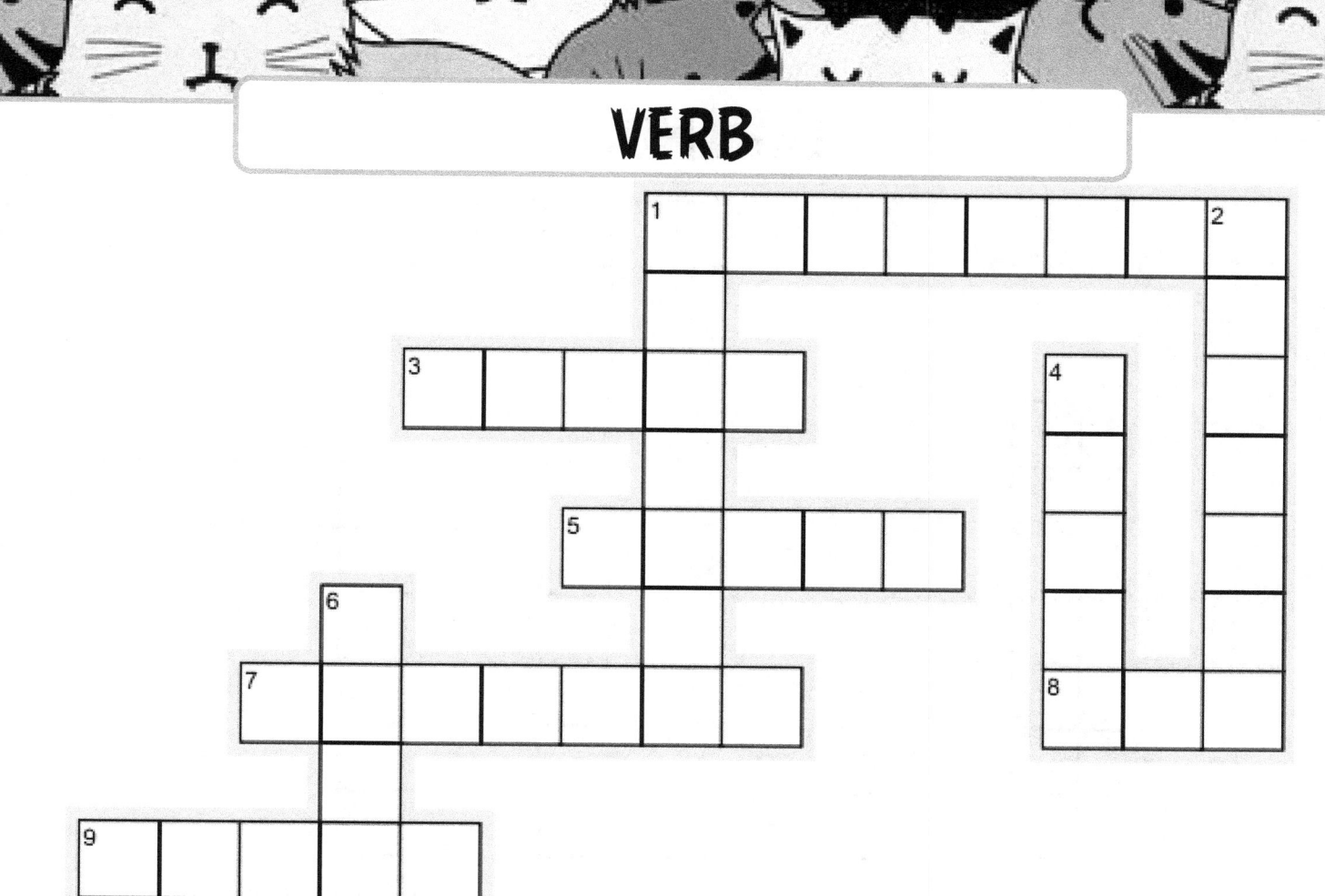

Across
1. To make friends with someone.
3. To take in marriage; take as one's husband or wife.
5. To take from one place to another; bear or support while moving; transport.
7. The act of pulling; applying force to move something toward or with you
8. To make a hole by removing dirt, sand, or the like.
9. Cleanse the entire body

Down
1. Negotiate the terms of an exchange
2. Make a mark or lines on a surface
4. To make by joining together different parts and materials; construct.
6. To use pressure against in order to move.

BIRTHDAY

Across

1. Very thin slices of fried potato that are eaten cold as a snack.
4. A sweet, frozen treat on a stick.
6. The tokens used for purchasing goods.
8. _____ bags - The items that people take away from a party, unusually some cake and a small thank you present.
9. The state of someone's body related to illness.

Down

2. Being able to do things without help.
3. To grow older and get better at something.
5. An unexpected event.
7. Something that you want to happen and ask for when blowing out candles on a birthday cake.
10. The time a person has lived, usually counted in years.

Conclusion

Thank you again for buying this book! I hope you enjoyed with my book. Finally, if you like this book, please take the time to share your thoughts and post a review on Amazon. It'd be greatly appreciated! Thank you!

Next Steps
– Write me an honest review about the book –
I truly value your opinion and thoughts and I will incorporate them into my next book, which is already underway.

Get more free bonus here

www.funspace.club
Follow us : facebook.com/funspaceclub

Send email to get answer & solution here : funspaceclub18@gmail.com

Find us on Amazon

Find us on Amazon

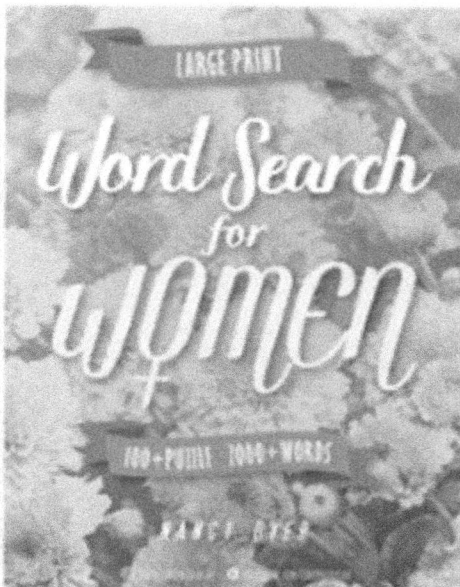

CPSIA information can be obtained
at www.ICGtesting.com
Printed in the USA
LVHW061459140321
681508LV00038B/840